100 DELICIOUS, EASY RECIPES
TO ENJOY TOGETHER

JOE'S FAMILY FOOD

JOE WICKS
THE BODY COACH

bluebird
books for life

JOE'S FAMILY FOOD

JOE WICKS
THE BODY COACH

First published 2021 by Bluebird
an imprint of Pan Macmillan
The Smithson, 6 Briset Street, London EC1M 5NR
EU representative: Macmillan Publishers Ireland Ltd, Mallard Lodge, Lansdowne Village,
Dublin 4

Associated companies throughout the world
www.panmacmillan.com

ISBN 9781529016314

3 5 7 9 8 6 4 2
A CIP catalogue record for this book is available from the British Library.
Printed and bound in Italy.

Publisher Carole Tonkinson
Project Manager Laura Nickoll
Project Editors Isabel Hewitt and Katy Denny
Senior Production Controller Sarah Badhan
Art Direction and Design Emma Wells and Nikki Dupin, Studio Nic&Lou
Food Styling Natalie Thomson and Katie Marshall
Prop Styling Charlie Phillips

Visit www.panmacmillan.com to read more about all our books
and to buy them. You will also find features, author interviews and
news of any author events, and you can sign up for e-newsletters

CONTENTS

SPEEDY SUPPERS

18. Chicken + mushroom pot noodle
20. Oaty katsu chicken dipppers
24. Chicken + avocado spaghetti
25. Fish goujon sandwich with beetroot Russian salad
28. Smoked haddock with creamy white bean mash + lemony greens
31. Salmon + broccoli fritters
32. Chicken + peanut butter noodles
34. Sesame-crusted salmon with greens
36. Speedy prawn + broccoli fried rice with egg crepe noodles
38. Spinach + ricotta tortellini soup
39. Roasted tomato pasta
40. Pea pesto on toast
43. Smoky chickpea jacket potatoes
44. Lemon + courgette puff pastry tart

THIS IS BANGING

46. Quick 5-spice tofu + vegetable noodles
48. Broccoli carbonara
52. Cheesy ham, mushroom + spinach rarebits

BUNG IT IN THE OVEN

56. Butternut + ricotta filo pie
58. Brussels sprout, red onion + chipolata traybake
60. Moroccan lamb meatball + roasted red pepper traybake with barley

62. BBQ Jerk chicken thighs with pineapple, black bean + spinach rice
64. Sweet potato cacciatore
65. Maple-glazed chicken thighs with Asian slaw
68. Garlicky BBQ spatchcock chicken with apple salsa verde + vegetable couscous
70. Cod, bean, tomato + rosemary parcels
72. Hasselback feta-stuffed broccoli with za'atar salmon fillets
75. Sumac chicken thighs with roasted black grapes + buttered couscous
76. Baked creamy sweet potato mash with sausages
78. Sweet potato rosti + salmon with basil yoghurt
79. Tomato, spinach + pepper gnocchi traybake
80. Rhubarb + strawberry frangipane tart
83. Chocolate, pear + oat breakfast traybake

ON THE HOB

86. Sausage + lentil ragu with polenta
88. Turkey pad Thai
90. Turkey meatball soup with broken pasta + vegetables
91. Mexican chicken burgers with corn salsa
94. Minted lamb with pomegranate salsa + garlic yoghurt
96. Cheesy cabbage + tofu Japanese-inspired pancakes
99. Honey + 5-spice chicken skewers with plum sauce

MY FAVOURITE

ROSIE'S FAVOURITE

100. Turkey tacos with guacamole
104. Lemon orzo chicken
106. Goan fish curry with green apple
108. Cod balls with tomato sauce + capers
109. Butternut squash, coconut + haddock chowder
111. Sweet potato gnocchi with buttered spinach + pine nuts
112. Chickpea + asparagus kedgeree
114. Beetroot risotto
119. Quinoa + spring vegetable minestrone soup
120. Green shakshuka with bacon + avocado
122. Chicken skewers with chickpea pepperonata

BIG BATCH

126. Lime leaf turkey meatballs with Thai red curry
128. Chana saag
131. Charred aubergine with spiced lamb
132. Aubergine pasta sauce
133. Tomato + lentil mascarpone pasta sauce
136. Lentil + kale hotpot
138. Kale + almond pesto
139. Big-batch hummus 3 ways
140. Butternut squash, bean + jackfruit chilli
142. Easy peasy fish pie pasta bake
144. Super-simple rosemary lamb stew

MEAT FREE

COOKING WITH KIDS

CELEBRATIONS

SKIM OVER THIS PAGE WHEN YOU NEED HELP CHOOSING WHAT'S FOR DINNER!

PAGE 25

PAGE 99

PAGE 193

PAGE 219

HELLO + WELCOME

TO JOE'S FAMILY FOOD

One of my favourite things in the world is sitting down with my family to enjoy wonderful home-cooked food. I think it's the perfect time to slow down, reconnect and check in with each other. Sometimes life seems to move at a million miles an hour and we can forget to actually enjoy and appreciate mealtimes. I remember dinnertimes being quite rushed as a kid, with lots of frozen food being thrown in the oven and then scoffed down as we watched *The Simpsons*.

As a parent now to two young children I've made a conscious effort to make sure cooking is something fun which we can do together and that dinnertime is calm and relaxed. For me personally, I feel it's a time to disconnect from screens and devices, reflect on our day and feel present in the moment. I can get so caught up in social media and work and find myself filming everything and sharing stuff if I have my phone with me so I've set myself a boundary that I don't have my phone during dinner, bath and bedtime with the kids. This has really allowed me to be so much more present and properly engage with everyone at dinner time. We try to create a calm environment when we eat, so we turn the TV off and listen to chilled and relaxing music, which helps.

I love getting Indie and Marley involved in the cooking, too, whether it's mixing some eggs for an omelette or adding some berries on top of their porridge at breakfast. I really do think the experience of adding ingredients and learning to create food is so important for young children. Of course, eating out in restaurants is fantastic but there is something extra special about home-cooked food. I feel like I appreciate it more when I've put some time and love into a meal and created it myself from scratch – and the kids love it too.

I think the key to stress-free cooking comes down to speed and simplicity, so all of the recipes in this book take that into consideration. I really think you and your family – no matter how big or small – will love each and every one of them.

Thank you so much for picking up my book and giving it a go. I'm so passionate about helping families eat healthier to feel happier and more energised, and I believe these recipes will do just that. Good luck with your first recipe. I would love to see what you make, so please tag me on Instagram or Twitter: @thebodycoach

LOTS OF LOVE, JOE

ROSIE, INDIE, MARLEY + ME

COOK'S TIPS

GET AHEAD

Meal planning when you have a family can make life a lot easier. Talk about it with your crew before you go shopping, and think about not just how much of each ingredient you need, but about balance, too, so you don't end up with a seven-day meat feast! All the ingredients in this book are really easy to get hold of.

SCALE TO SUIT YOUR FAMILY

A lot of the meals included here are for feeding a family of four (two adults, two small kids), but they can easily be scaled up or down, depending on how many people you're feeding. Just remember to tweak the cooking times if needed.

FREEZING, DEFROSTING + REHEATING

Make sure your dish is cool before you stash it in the freezer. It's worth dividing a dish into smaller portions before you freeze it, and don't forget to label it!

Defrost frozen food overnight in the fridge before reheating until piping hot. Once defrosted, heat and eat the food as soon as possible.

SPEEDY SUPPERS

QUICK + EASY MEALS...
MAXIMUM FLAVOUR,
MINIMUM PREP!

CHICKEN + MUSHROOM POT NOODLE

5 MINS / 10 MINS / SERVES 4 — 2 ADULTS + 2 SMALL KIDS

1 tbsp sesame oil
200g mushrooms, sliced
salt
300g dried instant noodles
 (try to find an Asian brand)
1 x 198g tin of sweetcorn,
drained
4 spring onions, thinly sliced
120g frozen peas
80g red or green cabbage,
 finely shredded
small bunch of coriander,
 roughly chopped
280g cooked sliced chicken

**FOR THE POT NOODLE
SEASONING**

3 tbsp brown miso paste
6 tsp dark soy sauce
½ tsp plus 2 pinches of soft
 or light brown sugar
3 tsp vegetable bouillon
 stock powder
1 tsp garlic paste
1 tsp ginger paste
3 tsp sesame oil
3 tsp tomato purée
1 lime, quartered

Put the sesame oil, mushrooms and a pinch of salt in a small frying pan over a medium heat and sauté the mushrooms for a couple of minutes until nutty brown and any water that has been released has evaporated.

Take 4 heatproof jars with lids (2 large jars for the adult portions and 2 medium jars for the kids' portions). In the bottom of each large jar place the following: 1 tablespoon brown miso, 2 teaspoons soy sauce, ½ teaspoon soft brown sugar, 1 teaspoon bouillon stock powder, ¼ teaspoon garlic paste, ¼ teaspoon ginger paste, 1 teaspoon sesame oil, 1 teaspoon tomato purée and the juice of ¼ lime. In each of the 2 smaller jars place the following: ½ tablespoon brown miso, 1 teaspoon dark soy sauce, a pinch of brown sugar, ½ teaspoon bouillon stock powder, ¼ teaspoon garlic paste, ¼ teaspoon ginger paste, ½ teaspoon sesame oil, ½ teaspoon tomato purée and the juice of ¼ lime.

Top each adult jar with 100g of dried instant noodles and each smaller jar with 50g, breaking the noodles into smaller chunks to fit. Divide the vegetables, coriander and chicken between the jars, adding slightly less to the smaller jars and packing everything down as you go.

When you are ready to eat your pot noodle, pour in enough freshly boiled hot water to just cover all the ingredients and quickly put the lids of the jars on. Leave the jars to sit for 4–5 minutes then shake gently to disperse the flavourings through the jar. Eat straight from the jar, using a fork and spoon, or pour the contents into a bowl if you prefer. (If serving straight from the jar for kids, make sure the jars aren't too hot before serving.)

You can assemble the jars ahead of time and store them in the fridge for up to 3 days, adding the hot water when you're ready to eat.

OATY KATZU CHICKEN DIPPERS

5 MINS / **15-20 MINS** / **FREEZE ME** / **SERVES 6**

4 ADULTS + 2 SMALL KIDS

olive oil spray
2 tbsp cornflour
salt and pepper
1 large egg, beaten
100g porridge oats
½ tsp smoked paprika
½ tsp garlic granules
380g chicken mini fillets

FOR THE KATZU SAUCE
1 tsp coconut oil
2 tsp mild curry powder
1 tsp garlic paste
1 tsp ginger paste
165ml tin coconut milk
1 heaped tsp dark roasted
 peanut butter
1 tsp honey
60ml apple juice
1 tsp cornflour mixed with
 1 tsp water

Preheat the oven to 220°C (200°C fan/gas mark 7), line a baking tray with foil and spray it evenly with olive oil spray.

Place the cornflour on a small plate and season with salt and pepper. Place the beaten egg in a small bowl and season with salt. Place the oats on another plate and mix with the paprika and garlic granules. Dust the mini fillets in the cornflour, then dip them in the egg, and finally roll the fillets in the oats to coat. Place them on your prepared baking tray.

Spray the top of the oaty fingers with an even coating of spray oil and bake in the oven for 15–20 minutes, or until cooked through and golden on the outside.

While the chicken cooks, make the katsu sauce. Heat the coconut oil in a small saucepan over a medium heat, add the curry powder and garlic and ginger paste and cook for 1 minute until fragrant. Add the remaining sauce ingredients, except the cornflour, and heat through until hot. Whisk in the cornflour mixture and allow to thicken a little before removing from the heat.

Serve the dippers with the sauce on the side.

SERVE WITH SALAD + RICE

CHICKEN + AVOCADO SPAGHETTI

5 MINS / 12 MINS / SERVES 4

2 ADULTS + 2 SMALL KIDS

PASTA COOKING WATER SHOULD BE AS SALTY AS THE SEA SO DON'T SKIMP ON THE SALT – IT WILL HELP MAKE THIS DISH SING!

250g wholewheat spaghetti
salt
80g frozen peas
2 tbsp olive oil
50g fresh breadcrumbs
grated zest and juice of 1 lemon
2 skinless chicken breasts, thinly
 sliced
2 large, perfectly ripe avocados,
 de-stoned and peeled (ideally
 Hass, as they are large and
 have super-creamy flesh)
3 heaped tbsp Greek yoghurt
½ tsp garlic powder
20g basil leaves
30g parmesan, grated
1 tsp smoked sweet paprika
 flakes
extra-virgin olive oil,
 for drizzling

Bring a large saucepan of water to the boil and season it generously with salt. Add the spaghetti and cook according to the packet instructions. Two minutes before the end of the spaghetti's cooking time, remove a cup of the pasta water and keep to one side, add the peas and cook for 1–2 minutes. Drain and return the peas and spaghetti to the saucepan.

While the pasta is cooking, heat 1 tablespoon of the olive oil in a frying pan over a medium heat, add the breadcrumbs and lemon zest and cook for 5–6 minutes until golden brown and crispy, moving them around in the pan to make sure they don't burn. Remove from the pan, set aside and wipe the pan clean.

Add the remaining tablespoon of olive oil to the frying pan, return it to the hob and turn up the heat. Add the sliced chicken and cook for 3–4 minutes until golden brown and cooked through.

Add the avocado flesh and yoghurt to a blender along with the lemon juice, garlic powder, three-quarters of the basil and the pasta water and blend until perfectly smooth.

Pour the avocado sauce over the pasta and peas, add the chicken and toss through. Using a pair of tongs, portion out the pasta. Sprinkle each serving with some of the crispy breadcrumbs, parmesan and smoked paprika flakes, drizzle over a little extra-virgin olive oil and tear the remaining basil over the top to serve.

FISH GOUJON SANDWICH WITH BEETROOT RUSSIAN SALAD

5 MINS / 10–12 MINS / FREEZE ME / MAKES 4   2 ADULTS + 2 SMALL KIDS

FREEZE GOUJONS BEFORE COOKING

Preheat the oven to 220°C (200°C fan/gas mark 7), line a baking tray with baking parchment, and spray it with olive oil spray to coat.

Season the beaten egg in a small bowl. Put the cornflour on a small plate and season with salt and pepper. Place the breadcrumbs and lemon zest on another plate. Dust the salmon strips in the seasoned cornflour, then dip each salmon strip in the beaten egg and, finally, coat in the breadcrumbs. Place the goujons on the lined tray and spray the tops with a little olive oil spray.

Bake the goujons in the oven for 10–12 minutes, or until cooked through and crispy on the outside, turning them halfway through the cooking time.

While goujons are in the oven, place the frozen peas in a small heatproof bowl and cover with just-boiled water. Leave for a couple of minutes until defrosted, then drain.

Put the drained peas, cubed beetroot, sliced radishes, spring onions, mustard powder, Greek yoghurt and chopped dill into a small mixing bowl and stir to combine. Season to taste with salt and pepper.

Butter the sliced bread and top with some of the watercress, two or three of the salmon goujons, then top with the Russian salad and remaining slices of bread, squashing everything down with the palm of your hand. Serve straight away.

olive oil spray
salt and pepper

FOR THE GOUJON SANDWICH
1 large egg, beaten
1½ tbsp cornflour
60g soft breadcrumbs
grated zest of 1 lemon
300g skinless salmon fillet, cut
 into 1.5cm (⅝in)-thick strips
butter, for spreading
8 slices of brown or seeded
 bread
2 handfuls of watercress

FOR THE RUSSIAN SALAD
60g frozen peas
160g shop-bought balsamic
 pickled beetroot, cut
 into small cubes
60g breakfast radishes, cut
 into 5mm (¼in)-thick slices
2 spring onions, thinly sliced
¼ tsp English mustard powder
130g Greek yoghurt
10g dill fronds, roughly chopped

PICTURED OVERLEAF →

FISH GOUJON
SANDWICH WITH
BEETROOT RUSSIAN
SALAD

SMOKED HADDOCK WITH CREAMY WHITE BEAN MASH + LEMONY GREENS

5 MINS / 10–15 MINS / SERVES 4 — 2 ADULTS + 2 SMALL KIDS

50ml olive oil, plus 1 tbsp and
 extra for greasing
3 anchovies in oil, roughly
 chopped
3 fat cloves garlic, thinly sliced
5 rosemary sprigs, needles
 stripped
4 x skinless smoked haddock
 fillets (2 x 120g per adult,
 2 x 70g per child)
80g garlic and herb soft cheese
1 tomato, cut into
 1cm (½in)-thick slices
30g cheddar, finely grated
100g trimmed cavolo nero,
 leaves roughly chopped
salt and pepper
1 lemon, halved
2 x 400g tins of cannellini
 beans, drained and rinsed
cooked green beans, to serve

Preheat the oven to 220°C (200°C fan/gas mark 7), line a baking tray with foil and lightly oil the tray.

Add the 50ml olive oil to a small saucepan over the lowest heat possible along with the anchovies, 2 of the sliced cloves of garlic and the rosemary needles and leave to infuse over the heat while preparing the rest of the dish.

Place the haddock fillets on the oiled tray and spread with the soft cheese. Top with the sliced tomato and sprinkle with the grated cheese. Bake in the oven for 10–15 minutes until the cheese has melted and the fish is cooked through.

Heat the tablespoon of olive oil in a large frying pan over a low heat, add the remaining garlic and cook for 30 seconds until fragrant. Add the cavolo nero, stir to coat in the oil, and season with a good pinch of salt. Add the juice of half a lemon along with a splash of water, and turn up the heat a little. Sauté for 3–4 minutes until the liquid has evaporated and the leaves start to crisp up a little round the edges and wilt.

Just before taking the fish out of the oven, put the drained cannellini beans in a medium saucepan over a medium heat and stir to heat through, then remove from the heat and mash a little with a potato masher until you have a rough mashed texture. Pour in the infused oil and stir to combine, then season with salt and pepper and add a squeeze of lemon juice from the other half of the lemon to taste.

Serve the fish with the greens, mashed white beans and green beans.

SALMON + BROCCOLI FRITTERS

10 MINS / **6 MINS** / **MAKES 14**

Cook the broccoli in a saucepan of salted boiling water for 2 minutes, then drain and leave to steam dry for a minute or two. Blitz in a food processor until finely chopped then empty into a bowl.

Add the salmon, eggs, flour and dill to the food processor along with the lime zest and juice. Blitz until smooth. Transfer the mixture to the bowl of broccoli and season to taste with a little salt and pepper.

Heat a little coconut oil in a frying pan over a medium heat and spoon in tablespoons of the mixture, flattening each tablespoon down a little and cooking for 2–3 minutes before flipping and cooking for a further minute. Continue until all the mixture is used up. Cut the remaining half lime into wedges and serve on the side, with a salad.

150g broccoli crown
salt
2 x 213g tins of cooked salmon, drained, and any big bones and skin removed
2 eggs
2 tbsp plain flour
1 tsp dried dill
grated zest of 1 lime and juice of ½
pepper
coconut oil, for frying
salad, to serve

SERVE WITH YOGHURT, MAYONNAISE, SALSA OR A SWEET CHILLI DIP

CHICKEN + PEANUT BUTTER NOODLES

5 MINS / 10 MINS / SERVES 4 — 2 ADULTS + 2 SMALL KIDS

3 nests of dried noodles
 (about 190g)
1 tbsp coconut oil
3 skinless chicken breasts,
 thinly sliced
1 tsp garlic paste
1 tsp ginger paste
100g baby corn, cut
 into quarters
1 carrot, peeled and cut
 into ribbons with a peeler
100g mange tout, cut into
 thin strips
1 red pepper, deseeded and
 thinly sliced
½ red onion, thinly sliced
small bunch of coriander,
 roughly chopped, to serve

FOR THE PEANUT SAUCE
6 tbsp peanut butter (dark roast
 works really well with this)
2 tsp Marmite
juice of 1 lime
1 tsp ginger paste
1 tsp garlic paste
1 tbsp sesame oil
1 tbsp honey
60ml water

Cook the noodles in a medium saucepan of boiling water according to the packet instructions.

Bring a kettle of water to the boil. Drain the noodles in a colander over the sink, then pour the kettleful of hot water over the noodles to remove any starch and stop them from sticking together.

Whisk together the peanut sauce ingredients in a small saucepan.

Heat a wok over a high heat and when it starts to smoke add the coconut oil along with the chicken, garlic and ginger paste. Cook until the chicken has lost most of its pinkness, then throw in the vegetables. Continue to cook, moving everything around in the pan for 1–2 minutes until the chicken is fully cooked.

Gently heat through the peanut sauce in the pan until just hot.

Toss the cooked noodles through the stir-fried chicken and vegetables. Using tongs, plate the noodles and spoon over the peanut sauce. Sprinkle each serving with a little chopped coriander and serve.

SESAME-CRUSTED SALMON WITH GREENS

5 MINS / 8-10 MINS / SERVES 4 2 ADULTS + 2 SMALL KIDS

1 tbsp coconut oil, melted, plus a little extra for greasing the tray
3 salmon fillets (skin on or skinless, it's up to you), each about 120g
50g white sesame seeds
1 tbsp sesame oil
150g Tenderstem broccoli, cut into finger-length pieces
200g spring greens, shredded

FOR THE SAUCE
2 tbsp ketchup
1 tbsp Worcestershire sauce
1 tsp Dijon mustard
1 tbsp honey
½ tsp lemon juice

Preheat the grill to medium. Line a baking tray with foil and lightly grease the foil with oil.

Whisk together the sauce ingredients in a small bowl until well combined.

Cut one of the salmon fillets into 2 portions to make 2 child-sized portions. Tip the sesame seeds onto a small plate. Brush each piece of salmon with the melted coconut oil and press both sides into the sesame seeds to coat.

Place the salmon fillets on the lined and greased tray and grill for 8–10 minutes, flipping the fillets halfway through the cooking time to cook both sides, until the sesame seeds are golden and the salmon is cooked through.

While the salmon is cooking, heat the sesame oil in a wok over a high heat, throw in the broccoli and sauté for 1 minute, then add the spring greens along with a splash of water. Place a lid on the wok for 1 minute to steam the vegetables, then remove and stir-fry for a further minute.

Plate up the salmon and vegetables and drizzle over the sauce to serve.

SPEEDY PRAWN + BROCCOLI FRIED RICE WITH EGG CREPE NOODLES

5 MINS / 12 MINS / SERVES 4   2 ADULTS + 2 SMALL KIDS

1 tbsp coconut oil
250g broccoli, cut into
 small florets
1 red onion, thinly sliced
200g raw peeled king prawns
1 tbsp ginger paste
1 tsp garlic paste
2 x 250g packs of pre-cooked
 jasmine rice
2 tsp soy sauce
2 tbsp ketjap manis
1 lime, ½ juiced, ½ cut
 into wedges
4 spring onions, thinly sliced
50g salted peanuts, finely
 chopped

FOR THE EGG CREPE NOODLES
2 large eggs
pinch of salt
pinch of caster sugar
sunflower oil, for greasing

First, make the egg crêpe noodles. Whisk the eggs with the salt and sugar in a bowl. Heat a medium non-stick frying pan over a low to medium heat and wipe it with an oiled piece of kitchen paper. Add a third of the egg mixture to the frying pan and swirl to coat the pan, cook for 30 seconds– 1 minute, or until just set, remove from the heat and leave to cool for a minute. Remove the crêpe from the pan and repeat with the remaining mixture. Roll up the crêpes, shred into thin 'noodles' and keep to one side for later.

Heat the coconut oil in a wok over a medium to high heat, throw in the broccoli florets and stir-fry for 2–3 minutes, or until starting to soften. Add the red onion, prawns, ginger paste and garlic paste and stir-fry for a couple of minutes until the onion is soft and the prawns are cooked through.

Heat the pre-cooked rice in the microwave according to the packet instructions, then add it to the wok along with the soy sauce, ketjap manis, lime juice and spring onions, and toss everything together.

Spoon the rice onto plates and top with the egg noodles and chopped peanuts. Serve with lime wedges on the side.

SPINACH + RICOTTA TORTELLINI SOUP

5 MINS | 20 MINS | FREEZE ME | SERVES 4

2 ADULTS + 2 SMALL KIDS

2 tbsp olive oil
2 tsp dried Italian herbs
1 celery stick, cut into
  5mm (¼in) cubes
2 small carrots, cut into
  5mm (¼in) cubes
1 onion, finely diced
1 courgette, cut into
  5mm (¼in) cubes
salt
1 tsp garlic paste
1 x 400g tin of chopped
  tomatoes
2 tbsp sundried tomato paste
1 tbsp sherry or red wine vinegar
800ml vegetable stock (made
  with 2 vegetable stock cubes)
1 x 300g pack of spinach and
  ricotta tortellini
80g trimmed cavolo nero or
  kale, leaves shredded

TO SERVE
pesto, to taste
grated parmesan
extra-virgin olive oil, for drizzling

Put the olive oil, Italian herbs, celery, carrots, onion and courgette in a large saucepan over a medium heat and season with a good pinch of salt. Cook for about 10 minutes, stirring from time to time, until the vegetables have softened.

Stir in the garlic paste and cook for another minute, then add the tinned tomatoes, sundried tomato paste, vinegar and stock and bring to the boil. Lower the heat and add the tortellini and shredded cavolo nero or kale and cook for a further 9–10 minutes, or until the pasta is cooked through.

Ladle into bowls and top with a blob of pesto, a grating of parmesan and a drizzle of extra-virgin olive oil to serve.

ROASTED TOMATO PASTA

5 MINS / 15 MINS / SERVES 4 — 2 ADULTS + 2 SMALL KIDS

Preheat the oven to 220°C (200°C fan/gas mark 7).

Place the cut tomatoes on a shallow baking tray, cut side facing up, and sprinkle with the garlic granules, brown sugar and red wine vinegar. Chop half the basil leaves and sprinkle them over too. Dot the butter over the tomatoes and season to taste with plenty of salt and pepper. Bake in the oven for 15 minutes until soft.

Meanwhile, cook the fresh pasta strips in plenty of salted boiling water according to the packet instructions. Remove quarter of a cup of pasta water before draining.

Toss the pasta with the extra-virgin olive oil, tip in the roasted tomatoes and toss everything together. Add the pasta water if it seems a little dry. Tear over the remaining basil leaves to serve.

600g best-quality cherry
 tomatoes, halved
¾ tsp garlic granules
1 tsp soft light brown sugar
1½ tsp red wine vinegar
small bunch of basil
45g butter
salt and pepper
350g fresh lasagne sheets, cut
 into 2cm (¾in)-wide strips
1 tsp extra-virgin olive oil

THIS IS BANGING WITH A SOFT POACHED EGG, GRATED PARMESAN + A ROCKET SALAD

PEA PESTO ON TOAST

2 MINS / 10 MINS / SERVES 1

100g frozen peas
15g toasted blanched almonds
2 basil sprigs
1 tbsp extra-virgin olive oil
a squeeze of lemon juice
1 tbsp grated parmesan
2 sundried tomatoes, finely
 chopped
salt and pepper

TO SERVE
slice of brown bread, toasted
1 soft-boiled egg
chopped cress – optional

Bring a kettle of water to the boil.

Place the peas in a heatproof bowl and cover with just-boiled water from the kettle and leave for 2–3 minutes, then drain.

Place half the peas in a mini chopper or food processor with the toasted almonds, basil, extra-virgin olive oil and lemon juice and blitz until smooth. Transfer to a bowl, stir in the remaining peas, grated parmesan and chopped sundried tomatoes and season to taste with salt and pepper.

Spread on toasted bread and top with a soft-boiled egg, halved, and some chopped cress, if you like.

SMOKY CHICKPEA JACKET POTATOES

2 MINS / 10 MINS / FREEZE ME / SERVES 4

2 ADULTS + 2 SMALL KIDS

SMOKY CHICKPEA MIXTURE ONLY

Heat the olive oil in a medium saucepan over a low to medium heat, add the onion, garlic, carrot and spices and season with a little salt and pepper.

Cook for 3–4 minutes until soft, then add the tinned tomatoes, chickpeas and balsamic vinegar and cook for a further 5 minutes.

Put the washed spinach in a microwaveable bowl, cover and zap on high for 1–2 minutes, until well wilted, or wilt in a dry pan. Remove and, as soon as it's cool enough to handle, squeeze out any excess water. Stir the spinach into the chickpeas.

Reheat your jacket potatoes in the microwave for 2–3 minutes, or until hot (or in the oven), split them down the middle and spoon in the smoky chickpea mixture. Top with the grated cheese and serve.

1 tbsp olive oil
1 onion, finely chopped
1 clove garlic, crushed
1 small carrot, grated
1½ tsp sweet smoked paprika
½ tsp ground cumin
salt and pepper
1 x 400g tin of chopped tomatoes
1 x 400g tin of chickpeas, drained and rinsed
1 tsp balsamic vinegar
200g spinach, washed
4 cooked jacket potatoes
200g cheddar, grated

TRY SWAPPING THE JACKET POTATOES FOR SWEET POTATOES.

YOU CAN COOK THE JACKET POTATOES AHEAD OF TIME.

LEMON + COURGETTE PUFF PASTRY TART

10 MINS / **15–20 MINS** / **SERVES 4** — 2 ADULTS + 2 SMALL KIDS

3 courgettes
small bunch of basil
grated zest of 1 lemon
1 clove garlic, crushed
salt and pepper
2 tbsp olive oil
1 x 320g packet of ready-rolled puff pastry (remove it from the fridge 15 minutes before needed)
2 tbsp sundried tomato paste
250g ricotta cheese
20g toasted pine nuts, to serve

Preheat the oven to 240°C (220°C fan/gas mark 9) and line a baking tray with baking parchment.

Using a speed peeler, peel the courgettes into ribbons and place the ribbons in a large bowl. Finely shred half the basil leaves and add them to the courgettes along with half the lemon zest, the crushed garlic, ½ teaspoon salt, some freshly ground black pepper and the olive oil. Toss everything together to evenly coat the courgette.

Unroll the pastry and place it on the lined baking tray. Using the point of a sharp knife, score a line 1cm (½in) from the edge all the way round the outside of the pastry to form a frame. Prick the inside rectangle of pastry a couple of times with a fork, then spread the inside rectangle with the sundried tomato paste. Add the courgettes, piling them on top and bake in the oven for 15–20 minutes, or until the courgettes are tinged golden brown and the pastry is cooked through.

While the pastry is cooking, mix the ricotta in a bowl with the remaining lemon zest and season with salt and pepper.

When the pastry is out of the oven, add blobs of the seasoned ricotta, scatter over the remaining basil leaves and sprinkle over the pine nuts to serve.

QUICK 5-SPICE TOFU + VEGETABLE NOODLES

5 MINS / **15 MINS** / **SERVES 4**

2 ADULTS +
2 SMALL KIDS

Cook the noodles in a medium saucepan of boiling water according to the packet instructions.

Fill your kettle and bring to the boil. Drain the noodles in a colander over the sink, then pour the kettleful of hot water over the noodles to remove any starch and stop them from sticking together.

Whisk together the sauce ingredients in a small bowl.

Mix the Chinese 5-spice, cornflour and salt and pepper together in a mixing bowl and toss the cubes of tofu in this mixture to coat.

Heat 1 tablespoon of the coconut oil in a wok over a medium heat and toss in the tofu, ginger and garlic pastes. Cook for 4–5 minutes until golden brown, then remove from the pan with a slotted spoon and keep to one side.

Add the remaining coconut oil to the wok, turn up the heat and throw in the vegetables. Stir-fry for 2–3 minutes until coloured but the vegetables still retain some bite.

Return the tofu to the wok along with the cooked noodles and move everything around in the wok to heat through a little.

Spoon the noodles and vegetables onto a large serving platter and drizzle over the sauce, tossing it through the noodles and vegetables. Sprinkle with the chopped cashews and roughly chopped coriander.

3 nests of dried egg noodles

FOR THE 5-SPICE TOFU
1 tsp Chinese 5-spice
1 tsp cornflour
½ tsp salt
pinch of freshly ground
 black pepper
300g firm tofu, patted dry and
 cut into bite-sized cubes
2 tbsp coconut oil
1 tsp ginger paste
1 tsp garlic paste
6 baby corn, each sliced into
 3 pieces
200g sugar snap peas, halved
200g radishes, cut into
 5mm (¼in)-thick slices

FOR THE SAUCE
5 tbsp light soy sauce
2 tbsp rice vinegar
2 tbsp tomato purée
3 tsp honey
juice of ½ lime

TO SERVE
70g toasted cashews,
 roughly chopped
handful of roughly chopped
 coriander

BROCCOLI CARBONARA

15 MINS / 15 MINS / SERVES 4 2 ADULTS + 2 SMALL KIDS

salt
1 head of broccoli, stalk
 removed
250g linguine
200g cubed pancetta
 (you can use either smoked
 or unsmoked)
2 cloves garlic, minced
4 egg yolks
freshly ground black pepper
50g parmesan, finely grated,
 to serve

KEEP THE BROCCOLI STALK, TRIM IT AND EAT IT RAW AS A SNACK, SLICED IN A SLAW OR ADDED TO A VEGETABLE SOUP.

Bring a large saucepan of generously salted water to the boil over a medium to high heat. Place the trimmed broccoli crown in the pan and cook for 3 minutes, then remove from the pan with a slotted spoon. Leave to steam dry for a minute.

Cook the pasta according to the packet instructions in the same pan you cooked the broccoli in, to save time and washing up.

While the pasta's cooking, put the broccoli in a food processor and blitz on pulse mode until finely chopped (or chop by hand).

Place a large frying pan over a medium to high heat and cook the pancetta for a few minutes until golden and its fat has been released. Lower the heat a little, add the minced garlic and cook for 1 minute until fragrant.

Drain the pasta, reserving a cup of the cooking water, and add the pasta to the frying pan. Continue heating and stirring for a minute to allowing the pasta to soak up the flavour of the pancetta and garlic.

Remove the pan from the heat and add some of the reserved pasta water (about three-quarters of a cup) and the egg yolks, and stir to create a creamy sauce. Don't be tempted to put it back on the heat or you will end up with scrambled eggs – the residual heat will gently cook the egg, creating a lovely glossy sauce. Add a little extra pasta water if it seems too dry.

Stir in the blitzed broccoli and season with plenty of black pepper (you shouldn't need to add any salt as the pancetta and parmesan are both salty). Sprinkle over the grated parmesan and serve.

CHEESY HAM, MUSHROOM + SPINACH RAREBITS

5 MINS / 12 MINS / 4 SLICES

2 tbsp butter
300g mushrooms, sliced
 (any variety)
salt and pepper
200g spinach, washed
1½ tsp plain flour
2 tbsp warm milk
180g cheddar, grated
1 tsp Worcestershire sauce
¼ tsp English mustard powder
4 slices of brown bread
4 slices of ham

THIS IS FAB WITH A FRIED EGG

Preheat the grill to medium.

Melt half the butter in a small frying pan over a medium heat, add the mushrooms with a pinch of salt and sauté for 5–6 minutes until most of the water released from the mushrooms has evaporated and they are nutty brown in colour.

Put the washed spinach in a microwavable bowl, cover and zap on high for 1–2 minutes until well wilted, or wilt in a dry pan. Remove and roughly chop as soon as it's cool enough to handle.

Melt the remaining butter in a small saucepan over a medium heat, add the flour and cook, stirring, for 2 minutes, before whisking in the warm milk until fully incorporated and smooth. Add the grated cheese, Worcestershire sauce and mustard powder and stir until the cheese has melted into the mixture and it has formed a thick paste. Remove from the heat and leave to cool a little while you toast the bread.

Place the bread slices on a baking tray and toast under the grill on one side before flipping and topping the other side with the ham, spinach and mushrooms, finishing with the cheese sauce. Place under the grill and cook for 4–5 minutes until golden brown.

BUNG IT IN THE OVEN

STICK EVERYTHING IN ONE DISH + BAKE. THAT'S ALL THERE IS TO IT!

BUTTERNUT + RICOTTA FILO PIE

20 MINS / **50 MINS** / **SERVES 5-6**

1kg butternut squash, peeled,
  deseeded and cut into
  1.5cm (⅝in)-thick slices
olive oil spray
salt and pepper
500g ricotta cheese
80g toasted walnuts, roughly
  chopped
3 eggs, beaten
grated zest of 2 lemons
1 tbsp dried sage
½ tsp garlic granules
270g filo pastry
green salad or cooked green
  vegetable of choice, to serve

Preheat the oven to 200°C (180°C fan/gas mark 6) and line a large baking tray with baking parchment.

Spray the sliced butternut with some olive oil spray to lightly coat, and season with plenty of salt and pepper. Place on the lined baking tray in a single layer. Roast in the oven for 20 minutes, or until cooked through and tinged golden brown.

Reduce the oven temperature to 180°C (160°C fan/ gas mark 4).

Whisk the ricotta cheese, walnuts, eggs, lemon zest, dried sage and garlic granules in a bowl.

Spray the inside of a 23cm (9in) loose-bottomed springform cake tin with olive oil spray. Spray a sheet of filo pastry with the olive oil and drape it over to line the bottom and sides of the cake tin. Continue this process, offsetting each sheet of filo and working your way around the cake tin, reserving the last sheet.

Add a layer of the roasted butternut squash to the base of the filo-lined tin, spoon in a layer of the ricotta mixture and continue layering until all the butternut and ricotta is used up.

Scrunch up the edges of the filo to cover the filling. Spray the final sheet of filo with olive oil spray and use it to fill in any gaps. Give the top of the pie a final spray with olive oil.

Bake in the centre of the oven for 30 minutes until golden brown and crisp and the ricotta is set inside.

Remove from the oven and leave to cool for 10 minutes before slicing and serving with a green salad or cooked green vegetables.

BRUSSELS SPROUT, RED ONION + CHIPOLATA TRAYBAKE

5 MINS / 40–50 MINS / SERVES 4

2 ADULTS + 2 SMALL KIDS

500g cooked new potatoes, large ones halved or quartered so all pieces are roughly the same size
12 chipolata sausages
400g Brussels sprouts, halved
100g bacon lardons
1 red onion, sliced into thick half-moons
salt and pepper
2 tsp fennel seeds
1½ tsp garlic granules
2 tbsp wholegrain mustard
1 tbsp olive oil
1 tbsp red wine vinegar
2 tbsp honey
small bunch of sage, leaves roughly chopped

Preheat the oven to 220°C (200°C fan/gas mark 7).

Arrange the potatoes, sausages, Brussels sprouts, bacon and red onion on a large baking tray and season with a little salt and pepper.

Bash the fennel seeds a little in a mortar and pestle until coarsely crushed, then sprinkle them over the tray.

Whisk together the garlic granules, wholegrain mustard, olive oil, red wine vinegar, honey and sage. Drizzle this mixture over the ingredients in the tray.

Place the tray in the oven and bake for 40–50 minutes, tossing everything after 20 minutes and putting the tray back in the oven until everything is well browned and cooked through.

Remove from the oven and serve.

If you have leftovers, make them into a sandwich: chop the sausages and mash the rest of the ingredients with the juices using a fork. Toast a brioche bun. Top one half with the mash, then add the sausages. Pop the other half of the brioche bun on top and tuck in.

BOXING DAY VIBES!

MOROCCAN LAMB MEATBALL + ROASTED RED PEPPER TRAYBAKE WITH BARLEY

15 MINS / 25 MINS / SERVES 4 — 2 ADULTS + 2 SMALL KIDS

4 red peppers, halved, deseeded and cut into 1cm (½in)-thick strips
2 tbsp olive oil
salt and pepper
1 x 400g tin of cooked barley, drained and rinsed, or 100g dried pearl barley
1 tbsp runny honey
green salad and flatbreads, to serve – optional

FOR THE MEATBALLS
400g lamb mince
1 tbsp ras el hanout
1 small onion, grated
1 egg
small bunch of flat-leaf parsley, finely chopped, plus extra to serve

FOR THE MINT YOGHURT
small bunch of mint, leaves finely chopped
300g natural yoghurt
grated zest of 1 lemon

Preheat the oven to 220°C (200°C fan/gas mark 7) and line a baking tray with baking parchment.

Place the red peppers on the lined tray, drizzle with the olive oil and season with salt and pepper.

Scatter the barley over the peppers (if using dried barley, cook it according to the packet instructions, then rinse and scatter it over the peppers).

Thoroughly combine all the meatball ingredients in a medium bowl using a spoon or your hands.

Roll the mixture into golf ball-sized balls that weigh about 35g (the mixture should make 14 or 15 balls). Nestle the meatballs among the peppers and barley, evenly spreading them out around the tray, and drizzle with the honey. Bake in the oven for 20 minutes, or until the meatballs are browned and cooked through.

While the traybake is in the oven, combine the mint yoghurt ingredients in a small bowl.

Serve the traybake sprinkled with parsley, with the mint yoghurt on the side, and a green salad and flatbreads, if you like.

GET YOUR HANDS IN THERE WHEN YOU'RE MIXING THE MEATBALL INGREDIENTS.

BBQ JERK CHICKEN THIGHS WITH PINEAPPLE, BLACK BEAN + SPINACH RICE

20 MINS / 35 MINS / SERVES 4

2 ADULTS + 2 SMALL KIDS

Preheat the oven to 220°C (200°C fan/gas mark 7).

Combine the ingredients for the spice mix in a small bowl.

Place the chicken thighs in a bowl or shallow tray and coat thoroughly with the spice mix, using your hands to rub the chicken all over. Drizzle with 2 teaspoons of the olive oil and rub it into the chicken.

Place the thighs on a baking tray and bake in the oven for 30 minutes until deeply golden and cooked through – you can test if they are cooked through by piercing them with a knife and checking that the juices run clear.

While the chicken is cooking, drain the black beans in a sieve and rinse thoroughly under cold running water for a minute or two. Keep to one side.

Rinse the rice in a fine sieve under cold running water, then put it in a medium lidded saucepan. Cover with cold water – the water should sit 1cm (½in) above the level of the rice – and add a pinch of salt. Cover and cook over a medium heat for 15–20 minutes until the rice is tender (check and stir after 10 minutes). When the rice is cooked it should have absorbed all the water and be fluffy. If there is any remaining water you can drain this off. Keep the rice in the pan and set aside.

While the rice is cooking, wilt the spinach in a medium frying pan over a high heat with the remaining teaspoon of olive oil for 1–2 minutes. Keep to one side.

Stir the black beans, spinach and pineapple through the rice and put it back over the heat for 2 minutes to warm through. Season with salt to taste and serve immediately, with the BBQ jerk chicken thighs.

BBQ METHOD

Heat your barbecue, then sear the spiced and oiled chicken thighs on the centre of the grill, or the hottest part, until nicely coloured on both sides. Move the meat to the side of the barbecue (the indirect heat) and cover. Cook for about 30 minutes, or until the juices run clear.

4 skinless and boneless
 chicken thighs
3 tsp olive oil

FOR THE SPICE MIX
½ tsp ground cinnamon
1 tsp ground allspice
2 tsp dried thyme
1 tsp salt
½ tsp freshly ground
 black pepper
½ tsp smoked paprika
1 tsp garlic granules

FOR THE RICE
1 x 400g tin of black beans
80g basmati rice
salt
200g spinach, washed
250g fresh pineapple, diced

SWEET POTATO CACCIATORE

5 MINS / **50 MINS** / **SERVES 4** → 2 ADULTS + 2 SMALL KIDS

2 tbsp olive oil
2 small red onions, thinly sliced
5 cloves garlic, thinly sliced
salt
2 x 400g tins of plum tomatoes
2 bay leaves
1 tbsp red wine vinegar
100g green pitted olives
1 tsp dried mixed herbs
300ml vegetable stock (made
  with 2 tsp vegetable bouillon
  stock powder)
600g small sweet potatoes,
  washed, skin left on, and cut
  into 2.5cm (1in)-thick slices
200g feta, broken into
  small chunks
small bunch of flat-leaf parsley,
  roughly chopped

SERVE WITH
A GREEN SALAD
OR STEAMED
GREENS

Preheat the oven to 240°C (220°C fan/gas mark 9).

Heat the olive oil in a wide, shallow lidded casserole dish over a medium heat, then add the onions and garlic with a good pinch of salt and cook for 3–4 minutes until soft and translucent. Add the plum tomatoes, bay leaves, red wine vinegar, pitted olives, dried herbs and vegetable stock and bring to a simmer. Season to taste.

Remove from the heat and arrange the sweet potato slices in the casserole dish, over the tomato mixture, in a single layer. Cover and bake in the oven for 20 minutes.

After 20 minutes, remove the lid and scatter over the feta. Return to the oven and cook for a further 20 minutes, or until the sweet potato is tender and cooked through.

Sprinkle with the flat-leaf parsley and serve.

MAPLE-GLAZED CHICKEN THIGHS WITH ASIAN SLAW

10 MINS / 25-30 MINS / SERVES 4

2 ADULTS + 2 SMALL KIDS

Preheat the oven to 220°C (200°C fan/gas mark 7) and line a baking tray with foil.

Combine the miso, garlic paste, ginger paste, maple syrup, soy sauce and sesame oil in a bowl. Season the chicken with a little salt and massage the marinade into the chicken thighs.

Put the chicken on the lined baking tray and cook in the oven for 25–30 minutes until cooked through and the chicken is golden brown and sticky on the outside.

While the chicken is cooking, prepare the slaw. Combine the finely shredded cabbage with the grated carrot, sliced radishes and spring onions in a bowl. Mix together the lime juice and maple syrup, season with salt and pepper and toss through the slaw mix. Sprinkle with the sesame seeds and pomegranate seeds to serve.

Serve the chicken with the slaw on the side.

1 tbsp white or brown miso paste
1 tsp garlic paste
1 tsp ginger paste
2 tbsp maple syrup
1 tbsp low-sodium soy sauce
2 tsp sesame oil
salt and pepper
6 large skinless and boneless chicken thighs

FOR THE ASIAN SLAW
250g white cabbage, finely shredded
100g carrot, grated
handful of radishes, thinly sliced
4 spring onions, thinly sliced
4 tbsp lime juice
1 tbsp maple syrup
2 tbsp toasted sesame seeds
80g pomegranate seeds

SERVE WITH STICKY JASMINE RICE

PICTURED OVERLEAF →

MAPLE-GLAZED CHICKEN
THIGHS WITH ASIAN SLAW

GARLICKY BBQ SPATCHCOCK CHICKEN WITH APPLE SALSA VERDE + VEGETABLE COUSCOUS

30 MINS / 1 HOUR / SERVES 4 — 2 ADULTS + 2 SMALL KIDS

Preheat the oven to 220°C (200°C fan/gas mark 7) and line a large baking tray with greaseproof paper.

Place the spatchcocked chicken on the lined baking tray and rub it all over with the garlic granules, the tablespoon of olive oil and a teaspoon each of salt and pepper.

Place the chopped vegetables around the chicken, drizzle with olive oil, and sprinkle with more salt and pepper. Roast in the oven for 45 minutes–1 hour until golden and the juices run clear when you put a knife into the thickest part of the thighs.

While the chicken and vegetables are in the oven, make the apple salsa verde. Finely dice the apples (discarding the cores and keeping the skins on), then place them in a medium bowl with the lemon juice. Cover and set aside.

Place the rest of the salsa ingredients in a food processor and pulse until fine but not pesto consistency – alternatively, chop everything very finely by hand. Stir through the green apple and set aside (you shouldn't need salt as the capers will season it).

Prepare the couscous according to the packet instructions and keep it warm in the saucepan or bowl with a lid on.

Once the chicken and vegetables are cooked, cut the roasted vegetables into a large dice, add them to the couscous and stir thoroughly to combine. (If you prefer, leave the veg as they are.)

Serve the chicken and couscous immediately, with the salsa verde on the side.

BBQ METHOD

When your barbecue is hot and ready for cooking, sear the oiled, spatchcocked chicken on the centre of the grill, or the hottest part, until nicely coloured on both sides.

Move the meat to the side of the barbecue (the indirect heat) and cover with foil or a lid. Cook for 45 minutes– 1 hour, or until the juices run clear when you pierce the thickest part of a thigh with a knife.

In the last 15 minutes, toss the vegetables with the olive oil and salt and pepper, sear the vegetables on the direct heat of the barbecue until slightly charred and cooked through. You can also move these to the indirect heat once seared and replace the lid.

1 whole chicken (about 1.5kg), spatchcocked (ask your butcher to do this or buy it pre-spatchcocked)
1 tbsp garlic granules
1 tbsp olive oil, plus extra for drizzling
salt and pepper
2 red peppers, quartered and deseeded
2 small courgettes or 1 large, cut into 1cm (½in) rounds
2 small red onions or 1 large, peeled and cut into wedges
200g couscous

FOR THE APPLE SALSA VERDE
2 Granny Smith apples
juice of 1 lemon
large bunch of flat-leaf parsley
large bunch of basil
small bunch of mint
1 clove garlic
6 tbsp olive oil
1 tsp Dijon mustard
1 tbsp capers, rinsed

COD, BEAN, TOMATO + ROSEMARY PARCELS

10 MINS / **15 MINS** / **SERVES 4**

2 ADULTS +
2 SMALL KIDS

2 x 400g tins of cherry
 tomatoes
1 x 400g tin of cannellini
 beans, drained and rinsed
4 tsp Worcestershire sauce
1 tsp garlic granules
salt and pepper
3 tbsp olive oil
6 rosemary sprigs,
 needles picked
3 tbsp capers, rinsed
150g trimmed fine
 green beans
2 x 120g cod fillets plus
 2 x 80g cod fillets

*YOU WILL NEED
4 LARGE SQUARES OF
FOIL FOR THIS RECIPE.*

Preheat the oven to 220°C (200°C fan/gas mark 7).

Mix the tomatoes, cannellini beans, Worcestershire sauce and garlic granules in a bowl and season with salt and pepper.

Heat the olive oil in a small frying pan over a medium heat, then add the rosemary and capers and cook for about 1 minute until the rosemary and capers become fragrant and crisp up slightly.

Divide the tomato and cannellini bean mixture between the 4 squares of foil. Top with the green beans followed by the cod fillets. Season each cod fillet with a little salt and pepper. Top each piece of fish with the rosemary, capers and olive oil.

Scrunch the foil up to form sealed parcels and cook in the oven on a baking tray for 15 minutes until the fish is cooked through.

Remove from the oven and serve.

*LET THE PARCELS
COOL A LITTLE BEFORE
SERVING TO KIDS.*

HASSELBACK FETA-STUFFED BROCCOLI WITH ZA'ATAR SALMON FILLETS

10 MINS / 25 MINS / SERVES 4 — 2 ADULTS + 2 SMALL KIDS

2 medium heads of broccoli
salt
3 x 120g salmon fillets
olive oil, for drizzling
2 tsp za'atar
200g feta, crumbled
grated zest of 1 lemon and
 a little lemon juice
30g sundried tomatoes,
 finely chopped
25g flaked almonds
25g breadcrumbs
½ tsp garlic granules

SERVE WITH BOILED NEW POTATOES

Preheat the oven to 220°C (200°C fan/gas mark 7) and line a baking tray with baking parchment.

Trim the base of the broccoli heads to a short stump so the broccoli can sit upright, keeping the crown of the broccoli fully intact.

Bring a large saucepan of salted boiling water to the boil, add the broccoli heads, cover and cook for 4 minutes, then remove from the water and allow to steam dry for 5 minutes, shaking off any excess water.

Halve one of the salmon fillets to make two small kids portions. Season all the salmon fillets and drizzle them with a little olive oil, sprinkle with the za'atar and keep to one side for later.

Mix the feta in a bowl with the lemon zest, sundried tomatoes, flaked almonds, breadcrumbs and garlic granules. Add a squeeze of lemon to bring the mixture together a little.

Place the broccoli crowns on the lined baking tray and make 3 evenly spaced incisions in each crown (making sure you don't cut all the way through). Stuff the gaps with the feta mixture. Drizzle the broccoli generously with olive oil and roast in the oven for 5 minutes, then add the seasoned salmon fillets to the tray and cook the salmon and broccoli for a further 15 minutes.

Remove from the oven and serve.

SUMAC CHICKEN THIGHS WITH ROASTED BLACK GRAPES + BUTTERED COUSCOUS

20 MINS / **1 HOUR** / **SERVES 4**

2 ADULTS + 2 SMALL KIDS

Preheat the oven to 220°C (200°C fan/gas mark 7).

Mix the sumac, garlic granules, cumin, softened butter, olive oil and soft brown sugar together in a small bowl.

Season the chicken thighs generously and smear over the butter mixture. Arrange the chicken thighs on a large baking tray, nestling the bunches of grapes around the chicken in the tray. Roast in the oven for 1 hour, or until the chicken is cooked through and the skin is crispy.

Ten minutes before the chicken is ready, tip the couscous into a heatproof bowl and pour over the hot water or stock. Cover the bowl with cling film and leave for 5–10 minutes until soft. Add the butter and season with salt and pepper. Fluff the couscous with a fork.

Serve the chicken with the roasted grapes and couscous, spooning over the juices from the tray.

2 tbsp sumac
½ tsp garlic granules
1 tsp ground cumin
35g butter, softened
2 tbsp olive oil
1½ tsp soft brown sugar
salt and pepper
6 skin-on, bone-in chicken thighs
300g black grapes, broken into smaller bunches

FOR THE BUTTERED COUSCOUS

150g couscous
150ml hot water or vegetable stock made from bouillon or cube
1 tbsp butter

GO AHEAD + USE RED GRAPES IF YOU CAN'T FIND BLACK.

BAKED CREAMY SWEET POTATO MASH WITH SAUSAGES

15 MINS / **30 MINS** / **SERVES 4** — 2 ADULTS + 2 SMALL KIDS

6–12 sausages
800g sweet potatoes, peeled and roughly chopped into equal-sized chunks
salt
60g butter
¼ tsp ground cinnamon
1 egg yolk
60ml double cream
juice of ½ lime
60g pecan nuts, roughly chopped
3 rosemary sprigs, needles picked and finely chopped
¼ tsp smoked paprika
1 tbsp olive oil
2 tsp maple syrup
80g crumbled blue cheese or grated cheddar

SERVE WITH STEAMED GREENS

Preheat the oven to 200°C (180°C fan/gas mark 6).

Place the sausages on a large baking tray, prick each one with a fork and cook in the oven for 25 minutes, or until cooked through and well browned.

Meanwhile, cook the sweet potato chunks in a medium saucepan of salted boiling water over a medium heat for 10–12 minutes until soft, then drain and allow to steam dry in a colander for a minute or two. Place the sweet potatoes in a food processor with the butter, cinnamon, egg yolk, cream and lime juice and blitz until super smooth and whipped. Season to taste and pour into a baking tray, spreading the mash out into an even layer.

Combine the pecans, rosemary, smoked paprika, olive oil and maple syrup in a small bowl. Spread the mixture over the top of the sweet potato, sprinkle over the cheese and bake in the oven for 15–20 minutes until the cheese has melted and the top is golden and bubbling. Serve with the sausages.

SWEET POTATO ROSTI + SALMON WITH BASIL YOGHURT

15 MINS | 20 MINS | SERVES 4 — 2 ADULTS + 2 SMALL KIDS

3 tbsp olive oil, plus a little extra for greasing
3 x 130g salmon fillets
salt and pepper
800g sweet potatoes, peeled
½ tsp garlic granules
1 tsp fresh thyme leaves
50g parmesan, finely grated
1 lemon, cut into wedges

FOR THE BASIL YOGHURT
25g basil leaves
150g natural yoghurt

SERVE WITH A ROCKET SALAD

Preheat the oven to 240°C (220°C fan/gas mark 9) and line a large baking tray with baking parchment. Lightly oil the parchment.

Halve one of the salmon fillets to make two small kids' portions. Season the fish with salt and pepper.

Using a peeler, cut the sweet potatoes into ribbons. Put the ribbons in a large mixing bowl along with the garlic granules, olive oil, fresh thyme and grated parmesan and season well with salt and pepper.

Arrange 4 heaps of the sweet potato ribbons on the lined and oiled tray, with 2 piles slightly larger for the adults. Add the salmon to the tray, around the sweet potato heaps, and cook in the oven for 15–20 minutes, or until the salmon is cooked through and the sweet potato rosti have tinged brown edges.

Blitz the basil and yoghurt in a blender until combined, then season to taste.

Serve the salmon and rosti with the basil yoghurt drizzled over the salmon, and lemon wedges.

TOMATO, SPINACH + PEPPER GNOCCHI TRAYBAKE

10 MINS / **20-26 MINS** / **FREEZE ME** / **SERVES 4** → 2 ADULTS + 2 SMALL KIDS

Preheat the oven to 220°C (200°C fan/gas mark 7).

Heat the oil in a medium saucepan over a low to medium heat, then add the onion and garlic and sauté for 2–3 minutes until softened and fragrant. Add the carrot and paprika and cook for a further 2–3 minutes.

Stir in the tinned cherry tomatoes and bring to the boil, then stir in the peppers, red wine vinegar, spinach, basil, half the mozzarella pearls and all the gnocchi with 50ml of hot water. Season to taste with salt and pepper.

Tip the gnocchi mixture into a suitable ovenproof dish, dot with the remaining mozzarella pearls and torn bread, drizzle with a little olive oil, especially over the torn bread, and bake in the oven for 15–20 minutes until golden and the cheese is bubbling.

Remove from the oven and serve.

2 tbsp coconut oil or olive oil
1 large red onion, finely chopped
2 cloves garlic, crushed
1 carrot, finely grated
1 tsp smoked paprika
1 x 400g tin of cherry tomatoes
2 small peppers (yellow, red or orange, or mixed), deseeded and thinly sliced
1 tbsp red wine vinegar
2 handfuls of spinach, washed
small bunch of basil, leaves roughly chopped
150g mozzarella pearls
450g shop-bought potato gnocchi
salt and pepper
50g ciabatta or stale bread, torn into 3cm (1¼in) pieces
olive oil, for drizzling

RHUBARB + STRAWBERRY FRANGIPANE TART

10 MINS / **30 MINS** / **SERVES 6**

80g unsalted butter, softened
 at room temperature
80g golden caster sugar, plus an
 extra 2 tsp for sprinkling
2 eggs, beaten
¼ tsp almond essence
120g ground almonds
50g plain flour
pinch of salt
grated zest of 1 lemon
320g sheet of ready-made puff
 pastry (remove it from the
 fridge 15 minutes before
 needed)
300g rhubarb stalks, cut into
 2cm (¾in) pieces
150g strawberries, hulled
 and halved
30g flaked almonds
crème fraiche or Greek
 yoghurt, to serve

Preheat the oven to 210°C (190°C fan/gas mark 6) and line a baking tray with baking parchment.

Whisk the butter and the 80g sugar in a mixing bowl with an electric handheld whisk until pale and fluffy.

Whisk in the eggs and almond essence a little at a time, whisking after each addition, until fully incorporated. Fold in the ground almonds, flour, salt and lemon zest until they are also fully incorporated.

Unroll the pastry onto the lined baking tray and score a 2cm (¾in) border around the edge of the pastry with a sharp knife.

Bake the pastry in the oven for 12 minutes, or until lightly golden and puffed. Remove the pastry sheet from the oven and, using the back of a spoon, push down the inside rectangle of pastry.

Top the inside rectangle of pastry with the frangipane, spreading it out evenly. Arrange the rhubarb and strawberries on top of the frangipane, sprinkle over the remaining 2 teaspoons of caster sugar and scatter over the flaked almonds.

Bake in the oven for 20 minutes, or until the pastry is golden brown and the fruit has started to soften.

Remove from the oven and serve the tart with a dollop of crème fraiche or Greek yoghurt.

CHOCOLATE, PEAR + OAT BREAKFAST TRAYBAKE

5 MINS / 20 MINS / SERVES 3 — 1 ADULT + 2 SMALL KIDS

Preheat the oven to 220°C (200°C fan/gas mark 7).

Put half the tinned pear halves in a blender along with the eggs, cinnamon, cocoa powder, yoghurt and maple syrup and blend until smooth and combined.

Mix the blended pear mixture with the oats and pour into a small baking dish roughly 23 x 17cm (9 x 6½in). Arrange the remaining pear halves in the dish, pushing them down into the mixture. Dot with the chocolate and hazelnut spread and bake in the oven for 20 minutes, or until set.

Remove from the oven, sprinkle with the chopped hazelnuts and serve with a dollop of extra yoghurt on the side.

2 x 410g tins of pear halves (in natural juice), drained
2 small eggs
½ tsp ground cinnamon
1 tbsp cocoa powder
150g Greek or natural yoghurt, plus extra to serve
2 tbsp maple syrup
130g porridge oats
4 tsp sugar-free hazelnut and chocolate spread
handful of chopped, toasted hazelnuts, to serve

ON THE HOB

MINIMAL EQUIPMENT REQUIRED FOR BANGING HOB-TOP MEALS... BOSH!

SAUSAGE + LENTIL RAGU WITH POLENTA

5 MINS / 25 MINS / FREEZE ME / SERVES 4

2 ADULTS + 2 SMALL KIDS

RAGU ONLY

6 best-quality sausages
a little olive oil, for frying –
 optional
1 clove garlic, crushed
1 onion, finely chopped
2 medium carrots, grated
1 celery stick, finely chopped
1 tbsp fennel seeds, coarsely
 ground in a mortar and pestle
needles from 2 rosemary sprigs,
 finely chopped
1 x 400g tin of chopped
 tomatoes
200g passata
1 x 250g pouch of good-quality
 cooked puy lentils
salt and pepper
600ml milk
170g instant polenta
40g parmesan, grated

Squeeze the sausage meat from the skins of the sausages, keeping the meat and discarding the skins.

Heat a large frying pan over a medium heat, add the sausage meat and cook for a couple of minutes, breaking up the meat with a wooden spoon as you cook. If your sausages are on the leaner side, you may need to add a splash of oil to the pan, but most should start to release their own fat.

When the sausage meat is almost cooked, add the garlic, onion, carrot, celery, fennel seeds and rosemary and cook for a further 8–10 minutes until the vegetables have softened.

Add the chopped tomatoes, passata and lentils, season to taste and leave to blip away while you prepare the polenta.

Heat the milk in a medium saucepan until just boiling, then lower the heat and slowly trickle in the polenta, stirring as you go. Cook for about 2 minutes until the grains are cooked and the consistency is thicker. Stir in the parmesan and season to taste.

Spread the polenta out on plates or in bowls then top with the sausage ragu to serve.

TURKEY PAD THAI

10 MINS / 20 MINS / SERVES 4 → 2 ADULTS + 2 SMALL KIDS

200g flat rice noodles
130g trimmed green beans,
 cut into short lengths
2 tbsp sesame oil
500g turkey thigh mince
2 tsp ginger paste
2 tsp garlic paste
2 tsp Thai 7-spice
1 tbsp fish sauce
1 tbsp soft light brown sugar
80g radishes, thinly sliced
1 large carrot, cut into ribbons
 with a speed peeler
2 eggs, beaten
bunch of coriander, roughly
 chopped
bunch of mint, roughly chopped
80g toasted peanuts, roughly
 chopped
1 lime, cut into wedges, to serve

FOR THE PEANUT SAUCE
3 tbsp smooth peanut butter
1 tbsp low-sodium soy sauce
2 tbsp fish sauce
juice of 1 lime

ADULTS MIGHT FANCY SOME CHOPPED FRESH CHILLI

Cook the noodles according to the packet instructions, and cook the green beans in the same pan as the noodles, or in a separate pan of boiling water (depending on the noodle cooking time), for 3 minutes. Drain the noodles and beans in a colander. Pour a kettleful of hot water over the noodles to remove any starch and stop them from sticking together. Keep to one side for later.

To make the peanut sauce, whisk the ingredients together in a small bowl, adding a splash of water if needed, to loosen the mixture a little.

Heat 1 tablespoon of the sesame oil in large non-stick frying pan or wok over a medium to high heat, add the turkey mince, ginger paste, garlic paste, Thai 7-spice, fish sauce and the brown sugar, and cook for 7–8 minutes, moving the mince around in the pan until cooked through and slightly caramelized. Remove from the pan, cover and set aside.

Add the radishes and carrot to the pan with a splash of water and cook for 1 minute. Move the vegetables to the side of the pan and add the remaining sesame oil and the beaten eggs. Leave to cook, moving the egg around in the pan, until just set.

Add the cooked noodles, green beans and minced turkey to the pan, along with the peanut sauce and chopped herbs, folding everything together gently, and warm through for 2 minutes. Remove from the heat, sprinkle with chopped peanuts and serve with lime wedges on the side.

TURKEY MEATBALL SOUP WITH BROKEN PASTA + VEGETABLES

15 MINS | 15 MINS | FREEZE ME | SERVES 4

2 ADULTS + 2 SMALL KIDS

2 tbsp olive oil
1 leek, trimmed and thinly sliced
200g carrot, roughly chopped
2 celery sticks, thinly sliced
900ml chicken stock (made
  with 2 chicken stock cubes)
2 bay leaves
1 x 198g tin of sweetcorn,
  drained
60g spaghetti, broken into
  short lengths
juice of 1 lemon
small bunch of flat-leaf parsley,
  roughly chopped
grated parmesan, to serve

FOR THE MEATBALLS
500g turkey thigh mince
½ tsp garlic granules
1 tsp English mustard powder
1 tbsp dried sage
30g dried or fresh breadcrumbs
1 tsp fennel seeds
1 egg, beaten
salt and pepper

Combine the ingredients for the turkey meatballs in a mixing bowl, season with salt and pepper, then roll the mixture into meatballs about 3cm (1¼in) in diameter and set aside.

Heat the olive oil in a medium saucepan over a medium heat, add the leek, carrot and celery and cook for about 5 minutes until they start to soften. Add the stock, bay leaves, sweetcorn, broken spaghetti and meatballs to the pan, bring to a simmer and lower the heat a little. Cook for 8–10 minutes, or until both the meatballs and pasta are cooked.

Add the lemon juice and sprinkle with the chopped parsley. Season to taste with salt and pepper and serve with plenty of grated parmesan.

MEXICAN CHICKEN BURGERS WITH CORN SALSA

15 MINS / 10 MINS / SERVES 4

2 ADULTS + 2 SMALL KIDS

Place the chicken breasts and the halved chicken breast between two sheets of baking parchment or cling film and bash with a rolling pin to flatten to a thickness of around 1cm (½in). Place on a plate and season with a little salt and pepper. Sprinkle the chicken with the Cajun spice mix (being more generous with the spice mix on the adult portions if you like) and drizzle over the lime juice and oil.

Toast the cumin seeds for the salsa in a dry frying pan over a low heat for 1 minute, or until fragrant, then bash to a coarse powder in a mortar and pestle.

Mix the mayonnaise in a bowl with the chipotle sauce and lime juice and set aside.

Heat a griddle pan over a high heat or prepare a barbecue grill and cook the chicken for 3–4 minutes on each side until strong char lines appear and the chicken is completely cooked through. While the chicken's cooking, add the corn cobs to the same pan and cook until charred on all sides.

Remove the chicken and corn from the pan. Strip the charred corn from the cob using a sharp knife and mix it with the chopped tomatoes, toasted cumin seeds, coriander, lime zest and juice.

To assemble the burgers, spread the top and bottom of the toasted buns with the mayonnaise, place the lettuce and sliced avocado on the bottom of the bun, followed by the chicken and then the corn salsa. Place the top buns on, and serve.

OPEN A WINDOW OR RAMP UP THE EXTRACTOR FAN WHEN YOU'RE GRIDDLING - IT CAN GET SMOKY.

3 chicken breasts, 1 cut in half lengthways (this will be for the kids' burgers)
salt and pepper
3½ tsp Cajun spice mix
3 tsp lime juice
4 tsp olive oil

FOR THE CORN SALSA
½ tsp cumin seeds
2 corn on the cob
8 cherry tomatoes, roughly chopped
4 coriander sprigs, roughly chopped
grated zest of 1 lime and 2 tsp lime juice

FOR THE SPICED MAYONNAISE
6 tbsp mayonnaise
2 tsp chipotle paste (leave this out of the kids' burgers if they don't fancy it)
2 tsp lime juice

TO SERVE
4 toasted buns
a few baby gem lettuce leaves
2 ripe avocados, de-stoned, peeled and thinly sliced

SERVE WITH SWEET POTATO FRIES OR SWEET POTATO CRISPS (SEE PAGE 214)

PICTURED OVERLEAF

MEXICAN CHICKEN BURGERS
WITH CORN SALSA

MINTED LAMB WITH POMEGRANATE SALSA + GARLIC YOGHURT

15 MINS / 5 MINS / SERVES 4

2 ADULTS +
2 SMALL KIDS

MARINATE THE LAMB FOR
A COUPLE OF HOURS OR EVEN
OVERNIGHT IF YOU
HAVE TIME.

8 'lollipop' lamb cutlets or
 4 leg of lamb steaks
salt and pepper
1 clove garlic, crushed
10g mint, leaves finely chopped
1 tsp dried mint
2 tbsp olive oil
1 tsp red wine vinegar

FOR THE POMEGRANATE SALSA

300g pomegranate seeds (most
 supermarkets stock prepared
 pomegranate in small tubs)
10g mint, leaves finely chopped
10g flat-leaf parsley, leaves
 finely chopped
2 tbsp extra-virgin olive oil
grated zest and juice of 1 lemon

FOR THE GARLIC YOGHURT

80g natural yoghurt
1 tsp garlic granules
a squeeze of lemon juice

SERVE WITH
GREEN SALAD +
BOILED NEW POTATOES
OR GRIDDLED
FLATBREADS

Place the lamb in a non-reactive metal, plastic or glass bowl. Season generously with salt and pepper, then add the garlic, fresh mint, dried mint, olive oil and red wine vinegar and massage a little to coat the meat. Cover and leave in the fridge to marinate for 10 minutes.

To make the salsa, mix all the ingredients together and season to taste with a little salt and plenty of pepper.

To make the garlic yoghurt, mix the yoghurt with the garlic granules and season to taste with lemon juice and some salt and pepper.

Heat a griddle pan or barbecue grill and cook the marinated meat for 2 minutes on each side for medium-rare, or longer if you prefer your meat more well done. Remove from the pan and leave to rest for 5 minutes.

Plate the lamb with the pomegranate salsa and garlic yoghurt on the side.

CHEESY CABBAGE + TOFU JAPANESE-INSPIRED PANCAKES

15 MINS / **30 MINS** / **MAKES 2-4**

2 LARGE OR 4 SMALL PANCAKES: ENOUGH FOR 2 ADULTS OR I ADULT + 2 SMALL KIDS

4 tbsp coconut oil
2 tbsp mayonnaise (preferably from a squeezy bottle)
2 tbsp toasted sesame seeds

FOR THE PANCAKE BATTER
3 large eggs, beaten
1 tsp baking powder
100g plain flour
salt and pepper
150g trimmed Savoy cabbage, leaves shredded
80g cheddar, grated
200g firm smoked tofu, coarsely grated

FOR THE SAUCE
2 tbsp ketchup
2 tbsp Worcestershire sauce
1 tsp Dijon mustard
1 tbsp honey
1 tsp lemon juice

SERVE WITH CHILLI SAUCE, IF YOU FANCY

To make the pancake batter, put the beaten eggs, baking powder, flour and 100ml of cold water in a large mixing bowl. Season with a little salt and pepper and whisk until you have a smooth batter with no lumps.

Whisk the sauce ingredients in a separate small bowl and keep to one side for later.

Fold the shredded cabbage, grated cheese and smoked tofu into the batter until fully incorporated. You can swap the tofu for flakes of fish such as tuna, salmon or mackerel, or shred in some cooked chicken instead.

Heat 1 tablespoon of the coconut oil in a medium non-stick frying pan over a medium heat, ensuring the oil coats the base of the pan.

Spoon in half the batter and spread out to fill the pan (if making 4 smaller pancakes cook the batter in batches of 2 pancakes at a time). Press the batter down with a spatula to help form the pancakes and cook for 6–7 minutes, or until golden brown and crispy, before flipping to cook the other side for 5–6 minutes, adding another tablespoon of oil, until golden brown and crisp.

Repeat the process with the remaining batter.

Plate the pancakes, drizzle them with the sauce, then add a zigzag of the mayonnaise to each and sprinkle with the sesame seeds to serve.

HONEY + 5-SPICE CHICKEN SKEWERS WITH PLUM SAUCE

20 MINS / 25 MINS / SERVES 4

2 ADULTS + 2 SMALL KIDS

Season the chicken thighs with the Chinese 5-spice and a little salt and pepper in a bowl, drizzle with the oil, and toss everything together to evenly coat. If you're using wooden or bamboo skewers, soak them in water for 30 minutes before using, so they don't burn. Thread the meat onto 6 skewers (2 per adult, 1 per child), putting less on two of the skewers for the children's portions. Keep to one side.

Put the plums in a blender and blend until perfectly smooth, then strain through a sieve into a medium saucepan.

Add the remaining plum sauce ingredients to the saucepan, set over a medium to high heat and cook, stirring continuously, for 10 minutes until the mixture has thickened to a rich glossy sauce consistency. Turn off the heat and cover to keep it warm while you cook the chicken.

Heat a large griddle pan over a medium to high heat. When hot, add the chicken skewers and cook for 3–4 minutes on each side or until cooked through. Just before removing the chicken from the pan, drizzle over the honey and cook for a further 30 seconds. Remove from the heat and keep to one side.

Heat the coconut oil in a large lidded frying pan over a medium to high heat, then add the pak choy and garlic paste, tossing to coat it in the oil and garlic. Turn the heat down a little, clamp on a lid and cook for 3–4 minutes, tossing occasionally, until the leaves are well wilted but the stems are still crisp with some bite. Drizzle with soy sauce and remove from the heat.

Reheat the rice according to the packet instructions and serve alongside the chicken skewers, pak choy and plum sauce.

6 large skinless and boneless chicken thighs, cut into 4cm (1½in) cubes
1 tsp Chinese 5-spice
salt and pepper
1 tsp olive oil
1 tbsp honey
2 x 250g packs of pre-cooked jasmine rice, to serve

FOR THE PLUM SAUCE
8 plums, de-stoned and quartered
2 tbsp honey
1 tbsp ginger paste
2 tsp garlic paste
1 tbsp low-sodium soy sauce

FOR THE PAK CHOY
1 tsp coconut oil
150g small pak choy, quartered, or larger pak choy, cut into wide strips
1 tsp garlic paste
1 tbsp low-sodium soy sauce

YOU WILL NEED 6 SKEWERS FOR THIS DISH.

TURKEY TACOS
WITH GUACAMOLE

15 MINS / 12 MINS / SERVES 4

2 ADULTS +
2 SMALL KIDS

SOAKING THE ONIONS
HELPS TAKE AWAY SOME
OF THEIR 'BITE'.

1 tbsp coconut oil
400g turkey thigh mince
1 tsp garlic paste
leaves from 1 oregano sprig,
 roughly chopped
juice of 1 lime
1 tsp smoked paprika
1 x 400g tin of borlotti beans
 (in water)
8 soft tacos
1 baby gem lettuce, shredded
small bunch of coriander,
 leaves picked
80g feta, crumbled

FOR THE PINK ONIONS
1 red onion, thinly sliced
salt and pepper
juice of ½ lime
leaves from 1 oregano sprig,
 roughly chopped

**FOR THE CREAMY
GUACAMOLE**
1 perfectly ripe Hass avocado,
 halved, de-stoned and peeled
juice of ½ lime
¼ tsp ground cumin
1 tbsp sour cream or Greek
 yoghurt

Preheat the oven to 200°C (180°C fan/gas mark 6).

For the pink onions, place the red onion in a small heatproof bowl, cover with hot water and leave for 10 minutes.

Drain and season with a little salt and pepper. Add the lime juice and oregano, stir and keep to one side while you prepare the rest of the dish.

Heat the coconut oil in a large frying pan over a medium heat, add the turkey mince and fry for 4–5 minutes, breaking it up with a wooden spoon as it browns, until no pink remains. Stir in the garlic paste, oregano, lime juice and smoked paprika and cook for 30 seconds, then add the beans, along with the water from the tin, and cook for a further 10 minutes, allowing the flavours to mingle. Season to taste with salt and pepper.

While the mince is cooking, make the guacamole by mashing together the avocado flesh in a bowl with the lime juice, cumin and sour cream or Greek yoghurt. Season to taste with salt and pepper.

Warm the tacos in the oven or on the hob to serve. Serve the warmed tacos filled with the mince turkey, top with the shredded lettuce, coriander leaves, pink onions, guacamole and crumbled feta.

MY FAVOURITE THING IS A DATE NIGHT AT HOME, COOKING TOGETHER AND ENJOYING A GIN TON.

LEMON ORZO CHICKEN

10 MINS / 45 MINS / SERVES 4 — 2 ADULTS + 2 SMALL KIDS

4 skin-on, bone-in chicken
 thighs
salt and pepper
1 fennel bulb, trimmed and
 bulb roughly chopped
250g carrots, roughly diced
1 onion, finely chopped
10g oregano leaves, roughly
 chopped
2 celery sticks, roughly diced
2 cloves garlic, crushed
olive oil, for frying (if needed)
200g orzo
600ml chicken stock (made
 with 1 chicken stock cube)
grated zest and juice of 1 lemon
100g garlic and herb soft
 cream cheese
150g frozen peas
bunch of flat-leaf parsley,
 leaves roughly chopped

Season the chicken thighs well with salt and pepper. Heat a wide, shallow lidded casserole dish over a low to medium heat and add the chicken, skin side down. Cook for about 15 minutes, until the fat from the chicken is beautifully golden, with crisp skin. Remove the chicken from the pan and set aside.

Add the chopped fennel, carrots, onion, oregano, celery and crushed garlic to the pan with a generous pinch of salt and cook the vegetables in the chicken fat, adding a splash of olive oil if needed, for 10 minutes, or until soft and lightly coloured.

Stir the orzo into the pan, return the chicken to the pan skin side up, along with the stock, and add the lemon zest and juice. Cover and cook for a further 15 minutes, or until the pasta is cooked.

Stir in the cream cheese and peas and cook for a final 5 minutes, then remove from the heat, sprinkle with the chopped parsley and serve.

GOAN FISH CURRY WITH GREEN APPLE

10 MINS / 20 MINS / FREEZE ME / SERVES 4

2 ADULTS + 2 SMALL KIDS

1 tbsp coconut oil
1 white onion, finely chopped
2 tomatoes, roughly chopped
¾ tsp turmeric
1 tbsp ground coriander
1 tsp ground cumin
1 tbsp ginger paste
8 curry leaves – optional
1 x 400ml tin of coconut milk
small bunch of coriander, leaves
 roughly chopped and stems
 finely chopped
1 Granny Smith apple, cut
 into matchsticks (peeled or
 unpeeled, it's up to you)
400g firm, skinless white fish
 fillets, such as cod, haddock or
 hake, cut into large cubes
165g raw shelled king prawns
½ lime

TO SERVE
cooked rice
½ lime, cut into wedges

Heat the coconut oil in a wide, shallow lidded frying pan over a medium heat, add the onion and cook for about 5 minutes until soft, then add the chopped tomatoes and cook for a further 5 minutes. Add the dried spices, ginger paste and curry leaves (if using), turn the heat up a little and cook for 2 minutes until fragrant. Add the coconut milk, half-fill the empty tin with water and swirl it around to collect any remnants and add the water to the pan. Throw in the coriander stems and bring to a simmer.

Stir the apple matchsticks into the curry, then add the fish and prawns. Squeeze over the juice of the half lime, cover and simmer for 5 minutes.

Remove from the heat, take off the lid, scatter over the coriander leaves and serve with rice and lime wedges on the side.

COD BALLS WITH TOMATO SAUCE + CAPERS

20 MINS / 25 MINS / FREEZE ME / SERVES 4

2 ADULTS + 2 SMALL KIDS

2 tbsp capers
small bunch of flat-leaf parsley, roughly chopped

FOR THE COD BALLS
380g skinless cod fillets
2 tsp English mustard powder
1 tsp dried Italian herbs
1 egg
grated zest of 2 lemons
50g parmesan, finely grated
plain flour, for dusting
salt and pepper

FOR THE TOMATO SAUCE
4 tbsp olive oil
2 cloves garlic, thinly sliced
1 x 400g tin of chopped tomatoes

SERVE WITH PASTA, RICE OR MASHED POTATO

Put all the cod ball ingredients (except the flour) in a food processor, season with salt and pepper and blitz until just combined. Be careful not to over-mix as you don't want to end up with fish paste – a couple of pulses should do it. If you don't have a food processor, finely chop the fish, put it in a mixing bowl and mix the remaining ingredients in by hand.

Lightly dust your hands with flour then roll the fish mixture into about 22 walnut-sized balls. Set aside.

To make the tomato sauce, heat the olive oil in a wide, shallow casserole dish or deep frying pan over a low to medium heat, add the garlic and cook for a minute or two until fragrant and soft. Add the tinned tomatoes, fill the empty tin a quarter-full with water. Swill the water around the tin then out into the pan and season with salt and pepper. When the sauce is hot, turn the heat up to medium and arrange the cod balls in the pan. Cook for 15–20 minutes until the cod balls are cooked through and the sauce is enriched.

Sprinkle the cod balls with the capers and flat-leaf parsley and serve straight from the pan.

BUTTERNUT SQUASH, COCONUT + HADDOCK CHOWDER

2 MINS / 15 MINS / FREEZE ME / SERVES 4

2 ADULTS + 2 SMALL KIDS

Heat the coconut oil in a medium saucepan over a medium heat, add the onion and cook for a few minutes until soft and translucent. Stir in the curry powder and cook for a further 30 seconds until fragrant. Add the coconut milk, bay leaves and 300ml of boiled water to the pan, bring to the boil, then reduce the heat to a low simmer.

Add the haddock and butternut squash and cook for 5–6 minutes, or until the squash is cooked through and the fish has lost its opaqueness and is also cooked through.

Stir in the grated nutmeg and sweetcorn, season with salt and pepper and squeeze in lemon juice to taste.

Spoon into bowls and sprinkle with chopped parsley or coriander to serve.

1 tbsp coconut oil
1 large white onion, finely chopped
1 tsp mild curry powder
1 x 400ml tin of coconut milk
2 bay leaves
350g smoked haddock, cut into 5cm (2in) pieces
1 x 350g pack of cubed butternut squash (or peel a butternut squash and cut it into 2cm/¾in cubes)
½ tsp freshly grated nutmeg
1 x 198g tin of sweetcorn, drained
salt and pepper
½ lemon
small bunch of flat-leaf parsley or coriander, chopped, to serve

SWEET POTATO GNOCCHI WITH BUTTERED SPINACH + PINE NUTS

25 MINS / **15 MINS** / **FREEZE ME** / **SERVES 4**

2 ADULTS + 2 SMALL KIDS

THE GNOCCHI ARE FREEZABLE (PRE BOILING)

Prick the sweet potatoes for the gnocchi with a fork a couple of times, rinse under cold running water to dampen them a little and put in a microwavable bowl. Cover and zap on high for 8–10 minutes, or until perfectly soft and cooked through. Alternatively, cook the pricked sweet potato in the oven for 45 minutes at 220°C (200°C fan/gas mark 7).

Remove from the microwave and leave until they are cool enough to handle, then peel off and discard the skin. If you have a potato ricer, use this to mash the sweet potato flesh as this will help create a light fluffy texture, otherwise mash with a fork or potato masher.

Mix the sweet potato with the salt, egg yolks and flour in a small mixing bowl until fully combined into a dough. Try not to over-work the dough.

Dust a work surface with flour, then flatten the dough out into a round disc about 2cm (¾in) thick. Use a teaspoon to cut and shape the dough into small gnocchi pieces – don't worry about them looking too perfect.

Bring a large saucepan of salted water to the boil, add the gnocchi and cook for a couple of minutes until they rise to the top and float. Scoop the gnocchi out with a large slotted spoon and transfer to a bowl.

Heat the butter in a large non-stick frying pan over a medium heat and add the gnocchi to the pan. Cook the gnocchi in the butter for a minute or two until lightly caramelized and tinged light brown.

Add the pine nuts to the pan and cook until golden, then add the spinach and sprinkle with the garlic powder and nutmeg. Cook until the spinach just begins to wilt and season to taste with a little salt and pepper.

Spoon onto plates or into bowls and grate over some parmesan to serve.

30g butter
30g pine nuts
250g baby spinach, washed
½ tsp garlic granules
¼ tsp ground nutmeg
salt and pepper
parmesan, to serve

FOR THE GNOCCHI
600g sweet potatoes (skin on)
½ tsp salt
2 egg yolks
150g flour (preferably
 '00' flour, but plain will do),
 plus extra for dusting

I LIKE TO TOP THE GNOCCHI WITH CHUNKY CROUTONS, FRESH CHILLI AND A DOLLOP OF CREAMY YOGHURT.

CHICKEN + ASPARAGUS KEDGEREE

15 MINS / 20 MINS / SERVES 4 — 2 ADULTS + 2 SMALL KIDS

2 tbsp coconut oil
4 banana shallots, peeled, halved and thinly sliced
600g skinless and boneless chicken thighs, cut into bite-sized pieces
2 tbsp Korma curry paste
250g white basmati rice, rinsed in a sieve under cold running water until the water runs clear
100g creamed coconut block
2 bay leaves
4 eggs
200g asparagus spears, trimmed and halved
150g frozen peas
1 lemon, halved and ½ cut into wedges
small bunch of coriander leaves
natural yoghurt, to serve

Heat the coconut oil in a wide, shallow pan over a low to medium heat, add the shallots and cook for about 5 minutes until they are just starting to take on some colour.

Mix the chopped chicken with the curry paste to evenly coat. Turn up the heat just a little then add the chicken to the pan of shallots, stirring and cooking for 3–4 minutes, or until the chicken is cooked through and no longer pink.

Add the rice to the pan and stir to coat the grains of rice in the oil.

Add the creamed coconut block to a heatproof jug with 550ml of boiling water and stir until the block has dissolved into the water. Pour the coconut into the pan with the rice, add the bay leaves and cook for 10 minutes, then turn off the heat and cover with a lid for 5 minutes so the rice can absorb any remaining liquid.

While the rice is cooking, boil the eggs for 8 minutes in a small pan of simmering water. In another small pan of boiling water, cook the asparagus and peas for 3 minutes. Drain the vegetables and peel and halve the eggs.

Mix the vegetables through the rice, along with the juice of the half lemon and the coriander. Top with the halved hard-boiled eggs, spoon onto plates and serve with a blob of natural yoghurt and a wedge of lemon on the side.

BEETROOT RISOTTO

5 MINS / 20–25 MINS / SERVES 4

2 ADULTS + 2 SMALL KIDS

30g pumpkin seeds
30g sunflower seeds
2 tbsp olive oil
4 banana shallots, thinly sliced
1 litre vegetable stock (made
  with 2 vegetable stock cubes)
250g arborio rice
2 tsp garlic granules
560g cooked beetroot – not
  in vinegar (available in most
  supermarkets), coarsely grated
juice of ½ lemon
100g parmesan, finely grated

TO SERVE
80g Greek yoghurt
100g feta, crumbled
small bunch of flat-leaf
  parsley or dill, chopped

SWAP THE FETA FOR SMOKY FLAKED MACKEREL IF YOU FANCY.

Put the pumpkin and sunflower seeds in a small frying pan over a medium heat and toast for a couple of minutes until they begin to pop. Remove from the heat and keep to one side until later.

Heat the olive oil in a wide, shallow frying pan over a medium heat, add the shallots and cook for about 5 minutes until softened.

Pour the stock into a saucepan and set over a low heat to keep it warm.

Add the rice and garlic granules to the shallots and stir to coat the rice in the oil, toasting the grains for about 1 minute.

Stir half the grated beetroot into the rice in the risotto pan. Add the hot stock to the pan, a ladle at a time, letting each ladleful be absorbed by the rice before adding another, stirring and cooking for about 15 minutes until all the stock is used and the rice is cooked but still retains a little bite. The risotto should have a glossy, loose texture.

Stir in the remaining beetroot, the lemon juice and the grated parmesan and adjust the seasoning if needed.

Spoon onto plates or into a shallow bowls and dollop with the yoghurt, swirling it through the risotto a little with a spoon. Sprinkle with the feta, toasted seeds and chopped herbs to serve.

QUINOA + SPRING VEGETABLE MINESTRONE SOUP

10 MINS / 25 MINS / FREEZE ME / SERVES 4

2 ADULTS + 2 SMALL KIDS

Heat a large saucepan over a medium heat, add the pancetta and cook for about 5 minutes until it releases its fat and crisps up to a golden brown. Add the celery, garlic, courgettes, rosemary sprig and leek, stirring the vegetables to coat them in the pancetta fat, and cook for 5 minutes, or until softened. Add the potatoes, quinoa and stock to the pan, cover and cook for about 10 minutes, or until both the potatoes and quinoa are cooked.

Stir in the peas and broad beans and cook for a further 2 minutes.

Season to taste and stir through the roughly chopped herbs. Ladle into bowls to serve, and sprinkle with plenty of grated parmesan.

130g cubed pancetta (smoked or unsmoked)
2 celery sticks, thinly sliced
2 cloves garlic, thinly sliced
200g baby courgettes, roughly chopped
1 rosemary sprig
1 leek, trimmed and roughly chopped
2 medium potatoes, peeled and cut into 1cm (½in) dice
4 tbsp quinoa
1 litre vegetable stock (made with 2 vegetable stock cubes)
100g frozen peas
100g frozen or fresh broad beans
salt and pepper
small bunch of flat-leaf parsley, leaves roughly chopped
small bunch of basil, leaves roughly chopped
grated parmesan, to serve

GREEN SHAKSHUKA WITH BACON + AVOCADO

5 MINS / 20–25 MINS / SERVES 2–3

1 ADULT + 2 SMALL KIDS OR 2 ADULTS

200g bacon lardons (smoked/
  unsmoked, it's up to you)
4 spring onions, roughly
  chopped
1 tsp cumin seeds, coarsely
  crushed in a mortar and pestle
1 tsp garlic granules
150g cherry tomatoes, halved
2 tsp red wine vinegar
130g frozen peas
300g spinach, washed
4 eggs

TO SERVE
1 avocado, de-stoned, peeled
  and sliced or chopped
½ tsp smoked paprika
  flakes – optional
1 lime, cut into wedges
toasted tortillas or bread

SERVE WITH CHILLI SAUCE (FOR THE GROWN-UPS)

Place a large lidded frying pan over a medium heat then add the bacon lardons and cook for about 10 minutes until they have released their fat and crisped up nicely.

Add the spring onions, crushed cumin seeds, garlic granules and cherry tomatoes to the pan and cook for a further 2 minutes, stirring from time to time.

Add the red wine vinegar, frozen peas and spinach to the pan, stirring to wilt the spinach and defrost the peas. When the peas are cooked and the spinach has wilted, make four spaces in the pan for the eggs and crack in the eggs to fill the holes. Cook the eggs to your liking – placing a lid on the frying pan will help to cook the top of the eggs.

When the eggs are cooked, remove from the heat, top with the avocado and sprinkle with the smoked paprika flakes (if using). Serve with the lime wedges on the side to squeeze over, and toasted tortillas or bread.

CHICKEN SKEWERS WITH CHICKPEA PEPPERONATA

10 MINS / 35 MINS / FREEZE ME / SERVES 4

2 ADULTS +
2 SMALL KIDS

650g skinless and boneless
  chicken thighs, cut into
  4cm (1½in) cubes
2 tsp dried oregano
1 tsp dried mint
2 tsp garlic granules
1 tsp sweet paprika
2 tbsp olive oil
grated zest and juice of 1 lemon
salt and pepper

**FOR THE CHICKPEA
PEPPERONATA**

3 tbsp olive oil
1 large or 2 small red onions,
  thinly sliced
2 cloves garlic, thinly sliced
4 large peppers (any colour
  except green), halved, deseeded
  and thinly sliced
350g mixed colour cherry
  tomatoes
2 tbsp red wine vinegar
1 x 400g tin of chickpeas,
  drained and rinsed
handful of flat-leaf parsley,
  leaves chopped, to garnish

*YOU WILL NEED
6 SKEWERS
FOR THIS DISH.*

Place the chicken in a non-reactive metal, plastic or glass bowl along with the oregano, dried mint, garlic granules, sweet paprika, olive oil, lemon juice and zest. Season with some salt and pepper and mix together with your hands to evenly coat. Leave to marinate while preparing the pepperonata (you can leave it for a few hours, or even overnight in the fridge, if you like).

If you're using bamboo or wooden skewers, soak them in water for 30 minutes before using, so they don't burn.

Heat the olive oil in a wide, shallow lidded frying pan over a medium heat, add the red onions with a pinch of salt and cook for 5 minutes until softened, then add the garlic and cook for a further minute until fragrant. Lower the heat a little and add the peppers and tomatoes to the pan, cover and cook for 20 minutes to soften, checking from time to time to make sure the ingredients are not sticking to the bottom of the pan. Add a splash of water if it starts to look too dry.

Stir through the red wine vinegar and chickpeas, and season to taste with salt and pepper. Garnish with parsley.

Thread the marinated chicken onto 6 skewers. Heat a griddle pan or barbecue grill and cook the skewers for 10–12 minutes, turning them regularly, until they are cooked all the way through.

BIG BATCH

BIG BATCH, BIG TASTE. GET AHEAD FOR THE WEEK AHEAD, OR MAKE ENOUGH TO FEED A CROWD!

LIME LEAF TURKEY MEATBALLS WITH THAI RED CURRY

20 MINS / 40 MINS / FREEZE ME / SERVES 8

FOR THE MEATBALLS
12 fresh, frozen or dried
  lime leaves
1kg turkey thigh mince
6 banana shallots, finely diced
2 tbsp fish sauce
¾ tsp garlic granules
50g bunch of coriander,
  leaves picked and stems
  finely chopped
3 tbsp coconut oil

FOR THE RED CURRY SAUCE
1 tbsp coconut oil
2 tbsp garlic paste
2 tbsp ginger paste
4–6 tbsp red Thai curry paste
  (depending on how hot you
  want it)
3 x 400ml tins of coconut milk
3 tbsp fish sauce
8 fresh, frozen or dried
  lime leaves
400g trimmed green beans,
  cut in half
4 pak choy, stems and leaves
  separated, roughly chopped

First, make the meatballs. If you're using dried lime leaves, soak them in a bowl of hot water for 10 minutes to soften. Finely shred the lime leaves and place in a large mixing bowl with the turkey mince, shallots, fish sauce, garlic granules and finely chopped coriander stems. Mix together well with your hands, then use a tablespoon to shape the mixture into walnut-sized balls – it should make about 50 meatballs.

Heat the 3 tablespoons of coconut oil in a large frying pan over a medium heat and cook the meatballs in batches for 10–12 minutes per batch until they are all cooked through and lightly browned. Keep to one side while you prepare the sauce.

Heat the tablespoon of coconut oil for the sauce in a large saucepan over a medium heat, add the three pastes and cook for 1–2 minutes until fragrant. Pour in the coconut milk and fish sauce, add the lime leaves, and bring to a simmer, then lower the temperature a little and add the turkey meatballs and green beans. Cook for 6 minutes. Stir in the pak choy stems and cook for a further 2 minutes. Remove from the heat and stir through the pak choy leaves, allowing the residual heat to wilt them.

Spoon into bowls and sprinkle with the coriander leaves.

SERVE WITH COOKED RICE + LIME WEDGES

CHANA SAAG

15 MINS / 20 MINS / FREEZE ME / SERVES 6–8

500g passata
500g spinach, washed
4 tbsp coconut oil
3 onions, finely chopped
5 cloves garlic, crushed
2 tbsp grated fresh ginger
2 tsp white mustard seeds
2 tsp ground cumin
1½ tsp garam masala
1 tsp ground cinnamon
¼ tsp turmeric
3 x 400g tins of chickpeas,
 drained and rinsed
juice of ½ lemon
salt and pepper

TO SERVE
natural yoghurt
cooked basmati rice
flatbreads (shop-bought or
 see recipe on page 190)

Put the passata in a blender then add half the spinach and blend until smooth, adding a splash of water if needed, to help bring it together.

Melt the coconut oil in a large saucepan over a medium heat, add the onions, garlic and ginger and stir-fry for 3–4 minutes until soft, then add the spices and cook for 2–3 minutes until fragrant.

Add the chickpeas and cook for 5 minutes, stirring to coat them in the spices, then add the blended spinach and passata. Add a splash of water to the blender and swill it to help remove the mixture from the sides, add to the pan, cover and cook for 5 minutes. Add the remaining spinach in batches, letting it wilt in the pan with the lid on, until all the spinach has been added.

Add the lemon juice and season with salt and pepper to taste.

Serve topped with a dollop of natural yoghurt, alongside basmati rice and flatbreads.

CHARRED AUBERGINE WITH SPICED LAMB

20 MINS / 40–50 MINS / FREEZE ME / SERVES 8

If you have a gas hob, blacken the aubergines directly over the flame, moving them around with a pair of tongs until they are blackened on all sides and completely soft (this can take up to 20 minutes). Alternatively, place them under a hot grill set to its highest setting and grill for about 20 minutes until blackened on all sides (although you won't get quite the same smoky flavour).

Leave the aubergines until they are cool enough to handle, then peel away and discard the blackened skin. Roughly chop the aubergines and keep to one side for later.

Heat the olive oil in a large saucepan over a medium heat, add the onions and a generous pinch of salt and fry for 5–6 minutes until soft and tinged golden. Stir in the crushed garlic and cook for a further 1 minute, then stir in the spices and chopped aubergines and cook for 3–4 minutes, stirring to coat the aubergine in the spices.

Add the lamb to the saucepan and cook for 10–15 minutes until it is completely browned, breaking up the meat with a wooden spoon, then stir in the tomato purée and pomegranate molasses. Season to taste and cook for about 5 minutes.

To make the salad, mix the sliced red onion in a bowl with the parsley leaves and lemon juice and season generously with salt and pepper.

Warm the flatbreads and serve them with the lamb mince, onion salad, pomegranate seeds and crumbled feta.

3 aubergines
4 tbsp olive oil
2 red onions, finely chopped
salt and pepper
4 fat cloves garlic, crushed
2 tbsp sweet smoked paprika
2 tsp ground allspice
1½ tsp ground cinnamon
2 tsp ground coriander
2 tsp ground cumin
1kg minced lamb
4 tbsp tomato purée
3 tbsp pomegranate molasses

FOR THE ONION + PARSLEY SALAD

2 red onions, very thinly sliced
large bunch of flat-leaf
 parsley, leaves picked
juice of 2 lemons

TO SERVE

8 flatbreads (shop-bought, or
 see recipe on page 190)
the seeds from 1 pomegranate
300g feta, crumbled

AUBERGINE PASTA SAUCE

15 MINS / 40 MINS / FREEZE ME / SERVES 6-8

FREEZE THE SAUCE IN BATCHES

5 aubergines, cut into
  2cm (¾in) cubes
90ml olive oil
2 large red onions, roughly
  chopped
5 cloves garlic, crushed
2 tbsp red wine vinegar
2 x 400g tins of chopped
  tomatoes
150g pitted Kalamata olives,
  roughly chopped
50g sultanas
small bunch of flat-leaf parsley,
  roughly chopped
salt and pepper

SERVE WITH YOUR
FAVOURITE PASTA
+ EITHER CRUMBLED
FETA, GRATED PECORINO
OR PARMESAN

Bring a kettle of water to the boil.

Place the cubed aubergines in a large heatproof mixing bowl and pour over the kettle of freshly boiled water, making sure the aubergines are all under the water. Leave for 10 minutes, then drain.

Heat the olive oil in your largest saucepan over a medium heat, add the onions and soften for 6–8 minutes until lightly caramelized. Add the garlic and cook for a further minute until fragrant. Add the drained aubergines to the pan and sauté for 10–15 minutes until softened and lightly coloured. Stir in the vinegar, tinned tomatoes, olives and sultanas and simmer for 15 minutes.

After 15 minutes, sprinkle with the flat-leaf parsley. Season to taste with salt and pepper.

Serve with pasta, using a little of the pasta cooking water to loosen the sauce to a good consistency.

TOMATO + LENTIL MASCARPONE PASTA SAUCE

DILUTED TO A LOOSER CONSISTENCY, THIS ALSO MAKES A REALLY GREAT SOUP.

15 MINS / 30-35 MINS / FREEZE ME / SERVES 8

FREEZE THE SAUCE IN BATCHES

Heat the olive oil in a large saucepan over a medium heat, add the chopped onions and celery with a generous pinch of salt and cook for 5–10 minutes until softened and the onions are tinged golden round the edges. Stir in the garlic and thyme and cook for a further 1–2 minutes until fragrant.

Stir in the brown sugar and balsamic vinegar and cook for 2 minutes, stirring constantly, then add the tinned tomatoes, stock and lentils. Cover and cook for 15–20 minutes, or until the lentils are fully cooked through and soft. Remove from the heat, add the mascarpone and blend with a stick blender until smooth. Season to taste with plenty of black pepper and some salt and remove from the heat.

Serve with pasta of your choice.

6 tbsp olive oil
3 red onions, roughly chopped
4 celery sticks, finely chopped
salt and pepper
6 cloves garlic, crushed
small bunch of thyme, leaves picked
1 tbsp dark brown sugar
50ml balsamic vinegar
2 x 400g tins of chopped tomatoes
1 litre vegetable stock (made with 2 tsp vegetable bouillon stock powder)
300g red lentils
250g mascarpone

I LOVE SEEING MARLEY + INDIE ENJOYING NEW FOODS. COOKING WITH THEM REALLY HELPS THEM BE MORE ADVENTUROUS.

LENTIL + KALE HOTPOT

15 MINS / 1 HR 10 MINS / FREEZE ME / SERVES 6

500g white or chestnut
  mushrooms
4 tbsp olive oil
salt and pepper
1 large onion, thinly sliced
4 medium carrots, finely
  chopped
3 celery sticks, finely chopped
small bunch of thyme, leaves
  picked
4 rosemary sprigs, needles
  picked and finely chopped
2 tsp garlic granules
2 tsp cumin seeds
2 tsp sweet smoked paprika
  flakes
3 tbsp sundried tomato paste
3 tbsp Worcestershire sauce
1 vegetable stock cube
1 vegetable stock pot
70g shredded, trimmed
  cavolo nero
250g green lentils, rinsed
500g new potatoes, sliced
  into 5mm (¼in)-thick rounds
40g butter
50g parmesan, finely grated

Preheat the oven to 200°C (180°C fan/gas mark 6).

Put the mushrooms in a food processor and blitz until finely chopped.

Heat half the olive oil in a medium casserole dish over a medium heat, add the mushrooms and a good pinch of salt, and cook for 8–10 minutes, or until the water from the mushrooms has evaporated and they are nutty brown in colour. Remove from the pan and keep to one side.

Add the remaining olive oil to the dish along with the onion, carrots, celery, thyme, rosemary, 1¾ teaspoons of the garlic granules, cumin seeds and sweet paprika flakes and cook for about 5 minutes until softened, stirring from time to time.

Add the mushrooms back to the pan, along with the sundried tomato paste and Worcestershire sauce, and cook for 1 minute.

Fill a heatproof jug with 1 litre of just-boiled water, crumble in the stock cube and stock pot until dissolved, then add the liquid to the casserole dish, along with the cavolo nero and lentils, and stir to combine. Season with salt and pepper.

Arrange the sliced potatoes on top of the casserole, sprinkle with the remaining ¼ teaspoon of garlic granules and season with salt and pepper. Dot with the butter, cover and bake in the oven for 25 minutes.

Remove the lid and sprinkle with the grated parmesan. Place back in the oven without the lid for a further 30 minutes, or until the potatoes are cooked through and golden brown on top.

KALE + ALMOND PESTO

15 MINS / NO COOK / FREEZE ME / SERVES 8–10

250g trimmed kale
salt and pepper
150g toasted blanched
 almonds (look out for creamy
 Macedonian almonds)
350ml extra-virgin olive oil
2 cloves garlic
juice of 1 lemon
80g parmesan, finely grated

Blanch the trimmed kale in a saucepan of salted boiling water for 1 minute, then drain and cool in a colander under cold running water to keep the vibrant green colour.

Gather the kale into a ball and squeeze to remove the excess water, then place in a food processor with the remaining ingredients and blitz until smooth. Season to taste with salt and pepper.

Spoon into containers, keep what you need in the fridge, and freeze the rest. You can freeze it in ice-cube trays to make handy small portions.

SERVE WITH PASTA, ON PIZZA, ON SOUP, OR SPREAD ON TOASTED BREAD TO MAKE BRUSCHETTA

BIG-BATCH HUMMUS 3 WAYS

10 MINS / 1–1½ HOURS / FREEZE ME / MAKES 800G

↳ + 12 HOURS (OR OVERNIGHT) SOAKING

Put the chickpeas in a bowl, cover with cold water and leave to soak for 12 hours, or overnight, then drain.

Put the chickpeas in a large saucepan and fill with enough cold water to sit 1cm (½in) above the chickpeas. Stir the bicarbonate of soda into the water.

Bring the pan of chickpeas to the boil, skimming off any scum, and cook for about 1 hour with the lid slightly ajar. Keep a close eye on the water level, adding some more hot water if necessary to make sure the pan doesn't boil dry.

When the chickpeas are cooked they will be very soft and easy to break with a fork – the cooking time may vary depending on how old the chickpeas are, so be patient and cook them for longer if they are not really soft.

Drain off any excess water if there is any left at the end, and leave to cool, then divide into three roughly equal portions.

To make roasted carrot, ginger and turmeric hummus, preheat the oven to 220°C (200°C fan/gas mark 7). Cook the carrots in a saucepan of boiling water for 5 minutes, then drain and transfer to a small baking tray. Drizzle with the oil, season lightly and roast in the oven for 30 minutes until soft. Place a third of the cooked chickpeas in a food processor with the roasted carrots and remaining ingredients, including 1 teaspoon of salt, and blitz until smooth and creamy. Adjust seasoning to taste.

To make lemon and garlic hummus, process a third of the cooked chickpeas in a food processor with the remaining ingredients until smooth. Adjust seasoning to taste.

To make beetroot hummus, process a third of the cooked chickpeas in a food processor with the remaining ingredients until smooth. Adjust seasoning to taste.

Keep some of the hummus in the fridge and freeze the rest for future packed lunches and easy, healthy snacking. You'll never buy shop-bought hummus again!

500g dried chickpeas
1½ tsp bicarbonate of soda

ROASTED CARROT, GINGER + TURMERIC

2 medium carrots, roughly chopped
salt and pepper
1 tbsp olive oil
50g tahini
3 tsp ginger paste
juice of ½ lemon
½ tsp turmeric
1 tsp garlic granules

LEMON + GARLIC

juice of ½ lemon
50g tahini
1 tsp garlic paste
1 tsp salt

BEETROOT

150g cooked beetroot – not in vinegar (available in most supermarkets)
½ tsp garlic granules
juice of 1 lemon
50g tahini

BUTTERNUT SQUASH, BEAN + JACKFRUIT CHILLI

15 MINS / 40–45 MINS / FREEZE ME / SERVES 6–8

6 tbsp coconut oil
2 large onions, roughly chopped
6 cloves garlic, crushed
salt and pepper
1 tbsp ground cumin
1 tbsp ground coriander
2 tsp sweet smoked paprika
2 tbsp harissa paste
1 tbsp soft dark brown sugar
1 butternut squash, peeled,
 deseeded and cut into
 2cm (¾in) cubes
1 x 410g tin of jackfruit,
 drained and chopped into
 bite-sized pieces
2 x 400g tins of chopped
 tomatoes
2 x 400g tins of mixed beans,
 drained
juice of 1 lime

Heat the coconut oil in your largest saucepan over a medium heat. Add the onions and garlic and a generous pinch of salt, and cook for 5–6 minutes until softened. Add the dried spices and cook for 2 minutes until fragrant, then add the harissa paste and brown sugar and cook for a further 1 minute.

Add the cubed butternut squash and another generous pinch of salt, stir to coat in the spices and cook for 5 minutes, stirring regularly. Add the jackfruit and cook for 2 minutes, then add the tinned tomatoes and mixed beans and stir to combine. Fill one of the empty tomato tins with water, swilling it a little to collect any tomato residue from the tin, and add it to the saucepan. Cover and cook for 20 minutes until the butternut squash is tender, stirring regularly to make sure the mixture doesn't stick to the bottom of the pan. If the stew starts to look a little dry, add a splash more water.

Add the lime juice, season with salt and pepper to taste and serve.

SERVE WITH
FLUFFY QUINOA,
NATURAL YOGHURT
+ GRATED CHEESE

EASY PEASY FISH PIE PASTA BAKE

5 MINS / 50–60 MINS / FREEZE ME / SERVES 8

500g penne pasta
1.2 litres whole milk
4 bay leaves
2 tbsp Dijon mustard
½ nutmeg, freshly grated
1 tsp garlic granules
200g frozen peas
2 tbsp cornflour mixed with
 2 tbsp water
200g baby spinach
200g raw shelled prawns
25g chives, finely chopped
640g fish pie mix
salt and pepper
120g fresh breadcrumbs
200g parmesan, finely grated

Preheat the oven to 200°C (180°C fan/gas mark 6).

Find your largest heavy-based saucepan and add the pasta, milk, bay leaves, Dijon mustard, grated nutmeg and garlic granules to the pan. Set it over a low heat and heat the milk and pasta, stirring regularly, for 25–30 minutes, or until the pasta is cooked and the milk has thickened slightly with the starch released from the pasta. Remove the bay leaves.

Stir in the peas and cook for a further 2 minutes until defrosted, then stir in the cornflour mix and cook for another 4–5 minutes until the milk has thickened to a sauce-like consistency. Turn off the heat, add the spinach and stir until it has wilted. Add the prawns, chopped chives and fish pie mix to the sauce and stir to evenly distribute. Season with salt and pepper.

Spoon into a large baking dish (or divide the mix between smaller baking dishes so you can put some away in the freezer for another time).

Mix the breadcrumbs with the grated parmesan and top the fish pie evenly with the mixture.

Bake in the oven for 20–25 minutes until the fish and prawns are cooked through and the top of the pie has browned.

If you want to freeze one of the pies, wrap the dish in cling film, or use a disposable large foil tray with a lid. Remember to thoroughly defrost the pasta bake before baking, taking it out of the freezer and transferring it to the fridge the night before you want to cook it.

SUPER-SIMPLE ROSEMARY LAMB STEW

20 MINS / **2 HOURS** / **FREEZE ME** / **SERVES 10**

A MIXTURE OF LEG + SHOULDER MEAT WORKS BRILLIANTLY HERE

80g plain flour
salt and pepper
2kg diced lamb
7 tbsp coconut oil or olive oil
3 large onions, roughly chopped
4 celery sticks, sliced
6 large peppers (mixed colours),
 deseeded and sliced
10 cloves garlic, crushed
small bunch of rosemary
 sprigs, needles picked and
 roughly chopped
5 tbsp tomato purée
2 x 400g tins of cherry tomatoes
2 cinnamon sticks
1.8 litres lamb or beef stock

SERVE WITH CREAMY MASHED POTATO, GREEN BEANS, POLENTA OR COUSCOUS

Put the flour in a large mixing bowl and season with plenty of salt and pepper. Toss the lamb in the seasoned flour then transfer it to a plate, shaking off the excess flour. Keep the excess flour for later.

Heat 3 tablespoons of the oil in your largest heavy-based casserole dish (or non-stick pan) over a medium heat, add the chopped onions and cook for 5 minutes, stirring regularly, until golden and lightly browned. Add the celery and peppers, cover with a lid and cook for 5 minutes. Uncover and add the garlic and rosemary and cook for a further minute until fragrant. Remove from the dish and keep to one side for later.

Add the remaining 4 tablespoons of oil to the dish and find a large baking tray to help with the next stage. Turn up the heat to high and sear the flour-dusted meat in batches until well browned on all sides, removing the browned meat and keeping it to one side on the baking tray for later. Be careful not to overcrowd the dish – it's worth taking your time over this part of the process.

Deglaze the dish by adding 200ml of water and using a wooden spoon to scrape away at all the brown caramelization on the bottom of the pan.

Return both the meat and vegetables to the dish. Stir in the reserved excess flour, along with the tomato purée, and cook for 30 seconds, then add the tinned cherry tomatoes, cinnamon sticks and stock.

Simmer uncovered for 1 hour, stirring regularly to make sure the stew isn't sticking to the bottom of the dish and adding a splash of water if it's getting too dry. Discard the cinnamon sticks and season to taste.

MEAT FREE

NO-ONE'S GOING TO MISS THE MEAT WITH THESE FEASTS!

CHEESE + TOMATO GALETTE

15 MINS / 25 MINS / SERVES 4 — 2 ADULTS + 2 SMALL KIDS

3 large best-quality ripe
 tomatoes, cut into
 1cm (½in)-thick slices
salt and pepper
500g block of shortcrust pastry
plain flour, for dusting
2 heaped tsp Marmite
100g cream cheese
100g cheddar, grated
1 small egg, beaten
1 tbsp sunflower seeds
1 tbsp sesame seeds

SERVE WITH
A SIMPLE GREEN
SALAD

Preheat the oven to 200°C (180°C fan/gas mark 6) and line a baking tray with baking parchment.

Season the tomato slices with a little salt and lay them out on a couple of pieces of kitchen paper to absorb some of the juices, then place a couple more sheets on top and keep to one side while you roll out the pastry.

Lightly dust a clean work surface with flour, then roll out the pastry to a large square the thickness of a pound coin. Using the tip of a sharp knife, cut a large circle roughly 30 x 33cm (12 x 13in) in diameter.

Place the circle of pastry on the lined baking tray and carefully spread the Marmite on top of the pastry, leaving a 6cm border around the edge. Next, spread the cream cheese on top and then sprinkle over the grated cheddar. Remove the kitchen paper from the tomatoes and arrange them on top of the cheese, overlapping them in a circular arrangement to cover the cheese.

Fold the edges of the pastry up over the tomatoes to form a crust. Brush the edges with the beaten egg and sprinkle them with the seeds.

Bake in the oven for 25 minutes, or until the pastry is golden brown and the tomatoes are tinged with colour around the edges.

Remove from the oven and serve.

COURGETTE + POTATO ROSTI WITH SOFT-BOILED EGGS + ROASTED TOMATOES

15 MINS / 30 MINS / SERVES 4 — 2 ADULTS + 2 SMALL KIDS

Preheat the oven to 200°C (180°C fan/gas mark 6).

Place the grated courgettes in a clean tea towel and fold the towel around the courgette to form a ball. Squeeze as hard as you can, over the sink, to remove as much moisture as possible. Place the courgette in a mixing bowl and repeat the same process with the grated potatoes.

Add 1 teaspoon of salt, the onion granules, sage and flour to the courgette and potato in the bowl and mix to combine. Grind in plenty of pepper and toss everything with your hands.

Heat 1 tablespoon of the coconut oil in a medium non-stick frying pan over a medium heat, add half the courgette and potato mixture, and spread it out to fill the pan. Cook for a couple of minutes, then start to press and shape the mixture, pressing down lightly with a fish slice to form a flat cake. Cook the rosti for 10–12 minutes until golden brown on the underside (you can check the colour by using a knife to lift up the edge of the rosti).

Meanwhile, put the tomatoes in a small baking tray with ½ tablespoon of the coconut oil and a little salt and pepper, and roast in the oven for 8–10 minutes until they start to collapse.

Place a plate on top of the frying pan and invert the rosti onto the plate so its cooked side is facing up. Add another tablespoon of the coconut oil to the pan and slide the rosti back into the pan to cook the other side for a further 5–6 minutes until golden brown. Transfer to a plate and cook the remaining rosti mixture.

Meanwhile, cook the eggs in a pan of boiling water for 5–6 minutes, or until cooked to your liking, then cool under cold running water and carefully peel.

Heat the remaining coconut oil in a medium saucepan or frying pan over a medium heat, add the cavolo nero and a generous pinch of salt, and cook for 1 minute, then add the lemon juice and garlic granules and cook for a further minute or so until wilted and crispy round the edges.

Cut the rostis into quarters and plate up with the roasted cherry tomatoes and kale. Cut the eggs in half and place them on top of the rostis to serve.

2 medium courgettes, coarsely grated (about 500g)
850g baking potatoes, coarsely grated
salt and pepper
2 tbsp onion granules
1½ tbsp dried sage
2 tbsp plain flour
6 tbsp coconut oil
300g cherry tomatoes
4 eggs
120g trimmed cavolo nero, leaves roughly chopped
juice of ½ lemon
½ tsp garlic granules

IF YOU HAVE TWO FRYING PANS, YOU CAN COOK BOTH ROSTI AT THE SAME TIME.

INDIAN SPICED CHICKPEA BURGERS WITH CAULIFLOWER RAITA + MANGO CHUTNEY

20 MINS / 10 MINS / SERVES 4   2 ADULTS + 2 SMALL KIDS

1 x 400g tin of chickpeas, drained and rinsed
3 tsp shop-bought curry paste (korma works well)
grated zest of 1 lemon
10g coriander, stems finely chopped and leaves roughly chopped
½ red onion, finely chopped
80g breadcrumbs
1 tbsp coconut oil

FOR THE CAULIFLOWER RAITA
300g cauliflower
150g natural yoghurt
juice of ½ lemon
10g mint leaves, finely chopped
salt and pepper

TO SERVE
4 burger buns, toasted
4 tbsp mango chutney
4 lettuce leaves
4 tbsp shop-bought crispy fried onions

To make the burger mixture, place the chickpeas, curry paste, lemon zest and fresh coriander in a food processor and blitz until the mixture comes together. If you don't have a food processor you can mash the mixture with a fork instead.

Mix the red onion and breadcrumbs into the chickpeas and shape into 4 patties.

To make the raita, shave the raw cauliflower with a mandoline or sharp knife into thin slices and place in a bowl. Mix together the yoghurt in a bowl with the lemon juice and mint, season to taste with salt and pepper and fold into the cauliflower.

Heat the coconut oil in a large non-stick frying pan over a medium heat, add the burgers and cook for 3–4 minutes on each side, or until golden brown on both sides.

Assemble the burgers by spreading the base of the toasted buns with mango chutney, then topping with the lettuce followed by the chickpea patties. Pile the cauliflower raita on top of each burger and sprinkle with the crispy fried onions. Place the bun lids on top and squash down a little with the palm of your hand to serve.

LENTIL FRITTERS WITH A CRUNCHY RADISH SALAD

15 MINS / 15–20 MINS / SERVES 4   2 ADULTS + 2 SMALL KIDS

3 tbsp vegetable oil
juice of 1 lime
pinch of sugar
salt and pepper
1 tbsp coconut oil
mango chutney and natural
  yoghurt, to serve

FOR THE FRITTER BATTER
150g gram flour or plain flour
200g natural yoghurt
2 eggs, beaten
1 tsp salt
3 tsp curry powder
2 x 250g pouches of good-
  quality cooked Puy lentils
30g coriander, leaves roughly
  chopped and stems
  finely chopped
8 spring onions, finely chopped
a splash of milk – optional

**FOR THE CRUNCHY
RADISH SALAD**
½ tsp cumin seeds
200g radishes, quartered
½ red onion, thinly sliced
10 cherry tomatoes, quartered
5g mint leaves, roughly chopped

First, make the batter. Whisk the flour, yoghurt, eggs, salt and curry powder in a mixing bowl until smooth. Stir in the lentils, chopped coriander stems and spring onions. Loosen the mixture a little if necessary with a splash of milk – it should have a dropping consistency: a small amount of the mixture should fall from the spoon if gently shaken.

Whisk the vegetable oil with the lime juice and sugar then season with salt and pepper. Keep to one side.

To make the salad, lightly toast the cumin seeds in a dry frying pan for 1–2 minutes until fragrant, then bash them a little in a mortar and pestle to help release their flavour.

Mix the radishes, red onion, tomatoes, cumin seeds, coriander leaves and mint leaves together in a bowl. Toss over the oil and lime juice mixture and keep to one side.

Heat the coconut oil in a frying pan over a medium heat. Cook the lentil fritters in batches, spooning in heaped tablespoons of the batter and cooking for 2 minutes on each side until golden brown. Continue until all the batter is used.

Serve the fritters with the radish salad and some mango chutney and natural yoghurt (swirled together if you like) on the side.

BUTTER BEAN + SUNDRIED TOMATO BITES WITH GARLIC YOGHURT

15 MINS / 15 MINS / FREEZE ME / MAKES 16

2 ADULTS OR 1 ADULT + 2 SMALL KIDS

1 x 400g tin of butter beans, drained
1 clove garlic, roughly chopped
1 tsp ground cumin
80g spinach, washed
grated zest of 1 lemon
1 tbsp plain flour
1 x 250g pouch of cooked brown rice
salt and pepper
120g sundried tomatoes, finely chopped
1 tbsp coconut oil

FOR THE GARLIC YOGHURT
100g natural yoghurt
1 clove garlic, crushed
1 tbsp extra-virgin olive oil

SERVE WITH SALAD + PITTA BREADS

Place the butter beans, garlic, cumin, spinach, lemon zest, flour and half the rice from the pouch in a food processor along with a generous seasoning of salt and pepper and blitz until the mixture comes together.

Tip the mixture into a mixing bowl and add the sundried tomatoes and remaining rice, and stir to combine.

Taste a little of the mixture and adjust the seasoning if needed, then shape the mixture into 16 small patties.

Heat the coconut oil in a large non-stick frying pan over a medium heat and cook the patties in batches for 3–4 minutes on each side, or until tinged golden brown.

While the patties are cooking, mix the garlic yoghurt ingredients together in a bowl and season to taste.

Serve the bites with the yoghurt on the side.

CHEESY ORZO-STUFFED TOMATOES

20 MINS / **1 HOUR** / **SERVES 4** → *2 ADULTS + 2 SMALL KIDS*

Preheat the oven to 200°C (180°C fan/gas mark 6).

Slice off the tops of the tomatoes and keep them to one side. Scoop out the pulp and seeds inside the tomatoes and transfer to a bowl. Drizzle 1 tablespoon of the olive oil into the bottom of a baking dish, place the tomato shells in the dish and season the tomatoes with a little salt and pepper.

Place the tomato pulp in a blender, blend until smooth, then pass through a sieve to remove any of the bitter seeds, pushing the mixture through to keep all of the pulp and juices.

Heat 3 tablespoons of the olive oil in a large frying pan over a low to medium heat, add the onion, oregano and courgettes and cook for 5–6 minutes until softened, then add the garlic and cook for a further minute until fragrant.

Pour the strained tomato pulp into the frying pan along with the orzo and cook over a low-medium heat for 12–15 minutes until the pasta is cooked, stirring regularly to prevent the pasta from sticking. You may need to add a splash of water if the mixture is looking dry. Stir in the chopped basil and remove from the heat.

Spoon half the orzo into the bottom of the hollow tomatoes, add a slice of mozzarella, then spoon in the remaining pasta and top each with another slice of mozzarella. Put the tomato tops back on the tomatoes and drizzle over the remaining olive oil.

Bake in the oven for 35–40 minutes, or until the tomatoes have started to collapse and are wrinkled on the outside.

Remove from the oven and serve.

8 beef tomatoes
6 tbsp olive oil
salt and pepper
1 red onion, finely chopped
1 tbsp dried oregano
2 small courgettes, cut into 1cm (½in) dice
1 clove garlic, crushed
150g orzo
small bunch of basil, roughly chopped
2 x 125g balls of mozzarella, each ball sliced into 8

SERVE WITH A GREEN SALAD OR SOME GREEN BEANS ON THE SIDE

'TASTE THE RAINBOW' BBQ TOFU SUSHI RICE BOWL

20 MINS / 15 MINS / SERVES 4

2 ADULTS +
2 SMALL KIDS

Prep all your ingredients.

Cook the rice according to the packet instructions, then spoon it into a large bowl with a wooden spoon and sprinkle with the rice vinegar to season.

Mix the shredded cabbage with the lime juice and season with a little salt.

Whisk together the dressing ingredients in a small bowl.

Cook the edamame in a small saucepan of boiling water for about 5 minutes until cooked through, then drain and keep to one side.

Mix the mayonnaise in a small bowl with the sriracha sauce (if using).

Toss the tofu in the spices and garlic granules and season with a little salt and pepper.

Heat the coconut oil for the tofu in a frying pan over a high heat, add the tofu and fry for 6–8 minutes until tinged golden brown. Pour in the BBQ sauce and water mixture and cook for another minute, or until the tofu is sticky and glazed. Remove from the heat.

Have all the ingredients to hand to assemble your bowls. Spoon the sushi rice into four bowls, portioning out slightly less for the children's bowls. Arrange the vegetables (including the shredded cabbage and edamame), mango and BBQ tofu on top of the rice and drizzle over the dressing. Sprinkle with the spring onions, crispy onions and cashews. Put a blob of mayonnaise on each bowl and serve.

220g sushi rice
2 tsp rice vinegar
170g red cabbage, finely shredded (about ¼ cabbage)
juice of ½ lime
salt and pepper
100g frozen edamame
4 tbsp mayonnaise
1 tsp sriracha sauce – optional
½ cucumber, peeled, halved lengthways, deseeded, and cut into thick slices
1 medium carrot, peeled and cut into ribbons with a speed peeler
2 small, ripe avocados, de-stoned, peeled and cubed
5 radishes, sliced
1 perfectly ripe mango, de-stoned, peeled and cubed
2 spring onions, thinly sliced
2 tbsp shop-bought crispy onions
50g toasted cashews, roughly chopped

FOR THE BBQ TOFU
280g firm tofu, cut into bite-sized chunks
1 tsp sweet smoked paprika
pinch of chilli powder
1 tsp ground cumin
½ tsp garlic granules
1 tsp coconut oil
2 tbsp BBQ sauce mixed with 2 tbsp water

FOR THE DRESSING
40ml light soy sauce
1 tbsp sesame oil
juice of ½ lime
juice of 1 clementine
¼ tsp honey
½ tsp grated fresh ginger or ½ tsp ginger paste

DON'T BE FOOLED BY THE LONG INGREDIENTS LIST – THE RECIPE IS SUPER SIMPLE.

'ALL THE GREENS' FILO + FETA PIE

15 MINS / 1½ HOURS / SERVES 4

2 ADULTS + 2 SMALL KIDS (WITH PLENTY OF LEFTOVERS!)

20g butter
2 leeks, washed and thinly sliced
2 banana shallots, thinly sliced
2 cloves garlic, crushed
200g trimmed kale, leaves roughly shredded
200g spinach, washed
grated zest of 2 lemons
large bunch of flat-leaf parsley, finely chopped
small bunch of dill, finely chopped
small bunch of mint, leaves finely chopped
100g feta, crumbled
100g toasted walnuts, roughly chopped
salt and pepper
3 eggs, beaten
olive oil spray
200g filo pastry

Preheat the oven to 180°C (160°C fan/gas mark 4).

Melt the butter in a medium saucepan over a medium heat, add the leeks, shallots and garlic and sweat for about 5 minutes until soft and tinged golden. Remove from the heat and transfer to a large bowl then, using the same pan (no need to wash it), add the shredded kale and sweat for 2–3 minutes until it has lost its bite and turns a darker green colour. Transfer to the bowl containing the leek mixture.

In the same pan, wilt the spinach over a medium heat for about 2 minutes until just cooked. Place the spinach in a sieve and press with a spoon to remove any excess liquid.

Roughly chop the spinach, add it to the bowl of greens and mix until combined. Add the lemon zest, chopped herbs, feta and walnuts, then season to taste with salt and pepper. Finally, add the beaten eggs and stir until fully combined.

Spray a 22cm (8in) springform cake tin with the olive oil spray.

Unroll the filo pastry and take a sheet of the filo, spray with olive oil spray and place it oil side down into the tin, allowing the pastry to drape over the sides. Spray oil onto another piece of pastry and place it on top of the first sheet, off-setting and overlapping it. Continue this process with the remaining sheets of pastry, going round the tin, until all sides are covered with filo.

Spoon the filling into the filo-lined cake tin and carefully fold the overhanging filo on top, making sure it's well covered. Spray with a little more olive oil spray.

Place in the oven and cook for 50–60 minutes, until it's a deep golden brown and the pastry is crisp. Remove from the tin and cut into wedges to serve.

ONE-PAN MUSHROOM + KALE MAC AND CHEESE

10 MINS / 30-40 MINS / SERVES 4 — 2 ADULTS + 2 SMALL KIDS

Heat the coconut oil in a medium, shallow casserole dish or frying pan over a medium heat, add the mushrooms and thyme leaves along with a generous pinch of salt. Cook for 10–15 minutes, or until all their water has been released and evaporated. You can speed this process up a little if you like by tilting the pan and spooning off some of the liquid, instead of waiting for it to evaporate (reserve the mushroom juices and stir them into the cheese sauce, if you like).

Stir in the kale and garlic granules and cook for a minute or two until the kale has wilted, then remove the mixture from the pan and keep to one side for later.

Add the milk, macaroni and any mushroom juices (if using) to the pan and put the pan back over the heat, lowering the temperature a little. Cook the mixture for about 15 minutes, stirring regularly, until the pasta is cooked through (by this point the milk will have thickened with the starches from the pasta and formed a silky, creamy sauce).

Stir 200g of the grated cheese into the sauce along with the mustard. Return the mushrooms and kale to the pan and stir to combine. Preheat the grill to medium.

Sprinkle the top of the mixture with the remaining cheese and the breadcrumbs. Drizzle with the olive oil and place under the hot grill for about 5 minutes until the cheese has melted and the top is golden brown. Serve straight from the pan.

2 tbsp coconut oil
750g chestnut mushrooms, thickly sliced
small bunch of thyme, leaves stripped
salt
60g trimmed kale, leaves roughly chopped
½ tsp garlic granules
1 litre whole milk
350g macaroni
300g cheddar, grated
2 tbsp Dijon mustard
35g fresh breadcrumbs
1 tbsp olive oil

SWAPPING THE CHEDDAR FOR BLUE CHEESE IS A WINNER, OR TRY SWAPPING KALE FOR SPINACH.

ONE-PAN COURGETTE + ROASTED PEPPER LASAGNE

10 MINS / 25 MINS / SERVES 4

2 ADULTS + 2 SMALL KIDS

3 tbsp olive oil
2 small onions, finely chopped
1 celery stick, finely chopped
1 small carrot, grated
3 courgettes, cut into
  2cm (¾in) cubes
2 cloves garlic, crushed
1 x 400g tin of chopped
  tomatoes
1 tsp mixed dried herbs
1 x 400g jar of roasted
  peppers in brine, drained
  and thinly sliced
salt and pepper
350g fresh lasagne sheets,
  each sheet cut into 4
  smaller squares
2 x 125g balls of mozzarella,
  1 ball sliced and 1 ball cubed
30g bunch of basil, leaves
  roughly chopped, reserving
  a few leaves to garnish
250g ricotta cheese
60g parmesan, grated

Heat the oil in a shallow casserole dish or frying pan over a medium heat, add the onions, celery and carrot and cook for 5 minutes until tinged golden and soft. Add the courgettes, turn up the heat and cook for a further 5 minutes until beginning to soften and tinged golden brown. Stir in the garlic and cook for a further minute until fragrant.

Add the tinned tomatoes and dried herbs, fill the empty tin with boiling water and empty it into the pan. Add the sliced peppers, season to taste with salt and pepper, reduce the heat to medium and simmer for 10 minutes.

Preheat the grill to medium and stir the pasta squares, mozzarella cubes and chopped basil into the courgette and tomato mixture.

Tip the ricotta cheese into a small bowl and stir in the grated parmesan (don't break the ricotta up too much). Season with salt and pepper.

Top the lasagne with the ricotta mixture and sliced mozzarella. Place under the grill and cook for 5–10 minutes until golden brown and bubbling.

Remove from the grill and serve, garnished with basil.

CRISPY TACO CUPS WITH BAKED EGGS + SPICY BEANS

10 MINS / 12–15 MINS / MAKES 6

olive oil spray
6 medium tortilla wraps
1 x 395g tin of taco mixed beans
 in spicy tomato sauce or mixed
 beans in chilli sauce
6 eggs
salt and pepper
100g cheddar, grated
handful of chopped coriander
2 ripe avocados
juice of 1 lime
hot sauce, to serve – optional

Preheat the oven to 200°C (180°C fan/gas mark 6).

Spray a 6-hole muffin tray with a little olive oil spray. Cut the wraps into quarters and press two of the quarters into one of the greased holes in the muffin tray with the points pointing down towards the centre to form a cup. Repeat this process with the remaining quarters to form 6 cups.

Spoon the beans into the 6 cups, crack an egg on top of each, and season the top of each egg with a little salt and pepper. Sprinkle with the grated cheese.

Spray each cup with a little olive oil and bake in the oven for 12–15 minutes until the eggs are cooked to your liking.

While the eggs are cooking, de-stone, peel, slice and dice or smash the avocados, add the lime juice and season with a little salt and pepper.

Serve the egg cups with the avocado and sprinkle them with the coriander (adults may like to add hot sauce).

THIS IS SUPER FLEXIBLE: SERVE IT FOR BREAKFAST, BRUNCH OR LUNCH.

CHICKPEA MAYONNAISE SANDWICH

10 MINS / **NO COOK** / **SERVES 1**

Put half the tinned chickpeas in a small bowl and mash them with a fork to a rough broken texture.

Add the remaining whole chickpeas to the bowl along with the Dijon mustard, chopped parsley, finely chopped onion, mayonnaise, cornichons (if using), lime zest and lime juice. Season to taste with salt and pepper.

Lightly toast the bread and spread one slice with the chickpea mayonnaise. Top with the sliced beetroot, lettuce and remaining bread slice, and serve.

YOU CAN MAKE THE CHICKPEA FILLING UP TO 3 DAYS AHEAD.

1 x 215g tin of chickpeas, drained and rinsed
1 tsp Dijon mustard
2 flat-leaf parsley sprigs, finely chopped
½ small red onion, finely chopped
4 tbsp mayonnaise
3 cornichons, finely chopped – optional
grated zest of 1 lime and 1 tsp lime juice
salt and pepper
2 slices of bread
1 small pickled beetroot, sliced
handful of lettuce

COOKING WITH KIDS

TIME TO GET THE LITTLE ONES INVOLVED. DON'T WORRY ABOUT THE MESS!

'DECORATE YOUR OWN' BERRY, AVOCADO + BEETROOT SMOOTHIE BOWL

5 MINS / **NO COOK** / **SERVES 2-3** — 1 ADULT + 2 PRE-SCHOOL CHILDREN OR 2 ADULTS

150g frozen mixed berries
100g frozen avocado (available
 in most supermarkets)
1 small banana
350ml almond milk
2 Medjool dates, stones removed
30g porridge oats

TOPPINGS
2 tsp chia seeds
2 tbsp almond butter
2 tsp pumpkin seeds
fresh fruit of choice

Place the smoothie ingredients in a blender and blend until smooth and creamy. Pour into bowls and decorate with the toppings – you can let your child do this bit.

LEARN TO EMBRACE THE MESS. IT'S ALL PART OF THE FUN.

SWEET POTATO, BLACK BEAN + KALE TACOS

10 MINS / 30 MINS / SERVES 4   2 ADULTS + 2 SMALL KIDS

700g sweet potatoes, peeled and cut into bite-sized chunks
3 tbsp coconut oil
2 tsp ground cumin
1 tsp sweet smoked paprika
1½ tsp garlic granules
salt and pepper
100g trimmed kale, leaves roughly chopped
2 limes, 1 halved, 1 cut into wedges
1 x 400g tin of black beans, drained and rinsed
120g natural yoghurt
1 tsp chipotle paste
1 large avocado, de-stoned, peeled and cubed
8 corn or flour tacos, toasted or warmed, to serve

Preheat the oven to 220°C (200°C fan/gas mark 7).

Put the sweet potato chunks on a baking tray with 2 tablespoons of the coconut oil. Sprinkle over the cumin, smoked paprika and 1 teaspoon of the garlic granules, and season with some salt and pepper. Bake in the oven for 2 minutes to melt the coconut oil, then remove and toss together to coat the sweet potato properly in the oil and spices. Return to the oven for 30 minutes, or until soft and tinged golden brown.

When the sweet potato is almost done, melt the remaining coconut oil in a medium frying pan over a medium heat. Add the kale, along with the remaining ½ teaspoon of garlic granules and some salt and pepper, and cook for 2–3 minutes until the leaves start to crisp up, then squeeze in the juice of half a lime. Remove from the heat and keep to one side.

Mix the drained black beans in a bowl with the remaining juice of half a lime and some salt and pepper to taste.

Mix half the yoghurt with the chipotle paste in a separate bowl and leave the remaining yoghurt plain for the children's tacos.

Mix the kale, black beans and avocado through the sweet potato in the baking tray. Serve with the tacos and a dollop of the yoghurt, with the lime wedges on the side.

MACKEREL RICE PAPER WRAPS WITH HOISIN SAUCE

30 MINS / NO COOK / MAKES 8

50g vermicelli rice noodles
8 large rice paper wrappers
½ cucumber, cut into
  matchsticks
4 spring onions, cut into
  thin strips
80g radishes, thinly sliced
small bunch of coriander,
  leaves picked
small bunch of mint,
  leaves picked
1 baby gem lettuce, leaves
  separated and cut into
  wide strips
200g sweet-cured or
  smoked mackerel, broken
  into smaller pieces
3 tbsp hoisin sauce, to serve

SOMETIMES VAC-PACKED
MACKEREL HAS LARGER
BONES DOWN THE MIDDLE
OF THE FILLETS - CHECK
THEM BEFORE USING.

Cook the noodles in a medium saucepan of boiling water according to the packet instructions, then plunge the noodles into cold water and drain in a sieve, shaking the sieve to remove any excess water.

Gather together all the prepared ingredients – you need everything to be to hand and in one place.

Submerge one of the rice paper wrappers in a bowl of cold water (or hold a wrapper under cold running water, making sure both sides are wet). Place the wrapper on a board close to all your prepared ingredients. You can get your child to help with this – you will need to supervise at first as they might find it a little tricky.

Place some of the noodles, prepared vegetables and a little of the mackerel towards the edge of the wrap closest to you. Don't overfill the wrapper or it will be hard to wrap up.

Lift the edge of the wrapper nearest to you over the filling, fold in the side and roll up tightly using your finger to keep the filling in position. Continue this process with the remaining ingredients.

Serve the rice paper wraps alongside the hoisin sauce for dipping.

FRYING PAN PIZZAS 3 WAYS

15 MINS / **10 MINS** / **MAKES 2**

Preheat the grill to high.

CHILDREN WILL LOVE HELPING WITH THIS BIT.

Place the pizza base ingredients in a mixing bowl and mix together with a spoon. Use your hands to bring everything together into a dough. Tip the dough out onto a floured work surface and knead for 2 minutes.

Have a large non-stick frying pan with a heatproof handle to hand. Split the dough in two with a knife. Making sure your work surface is well dusted with flour, shape each dough portion into a circular disc then, using your fingertips, pat the dough out into a thin round large enough to fit into your frying pan. Lift the base into the frying pan. You can get your little ones to help with this.

GET YOUR KIDS TO HELP TOP THE PIZZAS.

Now the base is ready to cook. Top it with your chosen topping and cook for about 5 minutes over a medium heat, lifting up the edge of the pizza to check the base has a good golden colour before removing from the heat.

Once the base is cooked on the underside and you've checked it has a good colour, slide the frying pan under the hot grill for 3–4 minutes, or until the cheese is tinged golden and bubbling. Repeat the process with the second pizza base.

SPINACH + CHICKEN

Put the washed spinach in a microwavable bowl, cover and zap on high for 2 minutes, or until well wilted, or wilt in a dry pan. Place the spinach in a sieve and press it with a spoon to remove as much water as possible.

Roughly chop the wilted spinach and mix it in a bowl with the cream cheese, garlic granules and some salt and pepper.

Top the pizza base in the frying pan with the spinach, followed by the chicken and sprinkle over the cheese.

INGREDIENTS FOR 2 PIZZA BASES

260g plain flour, plus extra for dusting
1½ tsp baking powder
pinch of salt
250g natural yoghurt

MAKES 1 SPINACH + CHICKEN PIZZA

250g spinach, washed
100g cream cheese
½ tsp garlic granules
salt and pepper
100g cooked chicken, cut into bite-sized chunks
50g grated mozzarella

CONTINUED OVERLEAF →

MAKES 1 FENNEL SAUSAGE + BROCCOLI PIZZA

1 tsp fennel seeds
60g passata
½ tsp garlic granules
½ tsp dried oregano
salt and pepper
2 sausages
1 tsp olive oil
1 tsp grated lemon zest
juice of ½ lemon
50g Tenderstem broccoli
50g grated mozzarella

FENNEL SAUSAGE + TENDERSTEM BROCCOLI

Using a mortar and pestle, bash the fennel seeds a little until coarsely broken.

Mix the passata in a small bowl with the garlic granules, oregano and some salt and pepper to season.

Squeeze the sausages from the skin and discard. Break the sausage meat into small chunks.

Heat the olive oil in a small frying pan over a medium heat, add the sausage with the fennel seeds and lemon zest and cook, breaking the sausage up a little as you go, until the sausage meat is tinged golden brown. Add the lemon juice.

Place the broccoli in a microwavable bowl with a quarter cup of water, cover and zap on high for 3 minutes, or cook in a saucepan of boiling water or in a steamer for 3 minutes.

Top the pizza base in the frying pan with the passata, spreading it out with the back of a spoon, followed by the sausage and drained broccoli. Sprinkle over the cheese.

MAKES 1 MUSHROOM + CAVOLO NERO PIZZA

60g passata
½ tsp dried oregano
¾ tsp garlic granules
salt and pepper
1 tsp olive oil
5 chestnut mushrooms, thinly sliced
4 trimmed cavolo nero leaves, roughly chopped
juice of ½ lemon
50g grated mozzarella

MUSHROOM + CAVOLO NERO

Mix the passata in a small bowl with the oregano and half a teaspoon of the garlic granules. Season with some salt and pepper.

Heat the oil in a frying pan over a medium heat. Add the mushrooms with a pinch of salt and fry for 5–6 minutes, or until nutty brown.

Add the cavolo nero to the pan along with the remaining garlic granules and another pinch of salt. Stir to coat in the oil and cook for 1 minute. Add the lemon juice and cook for a further 1 minute until the leaves have wilted.

Top the pizza base in the frying pan with the passata, spreading it out with the back of a spoon, followed by the mushroom and cavolo nero. Sprinkle over the cheese.

SPICED COCONUT, CHICKPEA + MANGO TRAIL MIX

THIS IS A GREAT NUTRITIOUS SNACK FOR WHEN YOU'RE ON THE GO, AND IT'S NUT FREE!

5 MINS / **30 MINS** / **MAKES 500G**

Preheat the oven to 200°C (180°C fan/gas mark 6) and line a baking tray with baking parchment.

Pat and rub the chickpeas dry using a clean, dry tea towel or some kitchen paper.

Mix the paprika, cumin, maple syrup, chilli powder (if using), coconut oil, soy sauce and salt in a small bowl until fully combined.

Place the chickpeas on the lined tray and drizzle half the spice mixture over, then toss to evenly coat. Roast in the oven for 30 minutes.

Toss the coconut flakes in the remaining spice mixture and add to the tray of chickpeas for the final 3–4 minutes of cooking.

Mix the mango with the roasted chickpeas and coconut – you can get your children to help mix everything together. Store in an airtight container for up to 3–4 days.

1 x 400g tin of chickpeas, drained and rinsed
1 tsp sweet smoked paprika
1 tsp ground cumin
1 tsp maple syrup
pinch of chilli powder – optional
2 tsp coconut oil, melted
1 tsp low-sodium soy sauce
¼ tsp salt
50g flaked coconut
100g dried mango, snipped into small pieces with a pair of scissors

HOMEMADE FLOUR TACOS

20 MINS / **2–4 MINS** / **FREEZE ME** / **MAKES 12**

↳ *PER TACO*

360g plain flour
1½ tsp baking powder
250g natural yoghurt

GET YOUR CHILD TO HELP WEIGH OUT THE INGREDIENTS, MIX THE DOUGH AND ROLL OUT THE TACOS.

Sift 260g of the flour with the baking powder into a large mixing bowl. Add the yoghurt and mix together to form a dough, bringing it together at the end with your hands and kneading for a minute or two to form a springy dough.

Divide the dough into 12 roughly equal-sized balls.

Place the remaining flour in a bowl. Now it's time to roll out the dough. If you have a silicone baking mat you can use this, otherwise cut a large plastic sandwich bag in half to create two square sheets. Taking some of the flour from the bowl and dust the silicone mat or plastic sheets heavily, then dip a ball of dough into the flour to coat and place the ball on one half of the silicone mat or in the middle of one of the sheets of plastic. Next, using your fingers, pat the ball out into a flatter disc shape, dust the disc again and then fold the silicone over the top or place the second sheet of plastic on top of the disc. Roll the disc out until it's about 3mm (⅛in) thick and about 10–12cm (4–4½in) wide. Peel the taco away from the sheet of silicone or plastic and repeat with the remaining balls of dough, stacking the rolled-out discs between pieces of baking parchment. Do this bit yourself, as the peeling and stacking is tricky for little fingers.

Heat a non-stick frying pan over a high heat and cook the tacos one at a time for 1–2 minutes on each side: they will puff up a little and brown blisters will appear, and that's how you know they are ready.

Keep the tacos warm and serve with the topping of your choice. The cooked tacos will keep for up to 3 days in an airtight container, and longer in the freezer.

CHEESE + ONION PITTA CHIPS

10 MINS / **10–12 MINS** / **MAKES 48**

PLENTY OF CHIPS FOR DIPPING!

Preheat the oven to 200°C (180°C fan/gas mark 6) and line a large baking tray with baking parchment.

Cut the pitta breads in half using a sharp knife through the middle to create two ovals. Cut each oval into 3–4 interesting shapes with a pair of scissors (supervise kids if they are doing the cutting).

Combine the parmesan, garlic granules, onion granules, dried chives and salt in a bowl.

Place the pitta shapes in a bowl and spray with the olive oil spray, trying to make sure that they all get an even coating. Add the parmesan mix and toss together with your hands. You can get your little one to help with this.

Tip the pitta chips onto the lined tray and spread them out into a single layer. Bake in the oven for 10–12 minutes, flipping them over halfway through the cooking time, until golden and toasted.

Remove from the oven and leave to cool, then use for snacking or dipping. They will keep for up to 4–5 days in an airtight container.

6 white pitta breads
55g parmesan, finely grated
1 tsp garlic granules
2 tsp onion granules
2 tbsp dried chives
½ tsp salt
olive oil spray

GET THE KIDS TO CUT THE PITTAS INTO WHATEVER SHAPES THEY LIKE.

CASHEW COOKIE BALLS

15 MINS / **NO COOK** / **MAKES 25**

GET YOUR LITTLE ONES TO HELP YOU WEIGH OUT THE INGREDIENTS AND ROLL OUT THE BALLS.

150g unsalted cashews
50g sunflower seeds
130g porridge oats
50g coconut oil, melted
170g smooth cashew nut butter
 or other nut butter
25ml maple syrup
80g dark chocolate, cut into
 small chunks

Place the cashews, sunflower seeds and oats in a food processor and blitz until finely milled to a flour-like consistency.

Add the melted coconut oil, nut butter and maple syrup to the food processor and pulse until the mixture comes together into one lump.

Tip the mixture into a bowl and knead in the chocolate chunks to evenly distribute them.

Roll the mixture into about 25 walnut-sized balls.

Place the balls in an airtight container in the fridge. They will keep for up to 1–2 weeks.

CARROT + WALNUT BLISS BALLS

20 MINS / **NO COOK** / **MAKES 16**

100g carrot, finely grated
120g walnuts
100g sunflower seeds
1 tsp ground cinnamon
120g Medjool dates, stones
 removed
pinch of salt
30g desiccated coconut

Put all the ingredients, except the desiccated coconut, in a food processor and blitz until the mixture comes together into one lump.

Roll the mixture into about 16 balls. Place the desiccated coconut on a plate and roll the balls in the coconut until they are coated.

Place the balls in an airtight container in the fridge. They will keep for up to 1 week.

CARROT + WALNUT
BLISS BALLS

CASHEW
COOKIE
BALLS

PLUM FRUIT WINDERS

15 MINS / **2½ HOURS** / **1 SHEET**

ROUGHLY 25x35CM (10x14IN)

500g plums, halved and stoned
150g cooked beetroot – not
in vinegar (available in most
supermarkets)
honey

Preheat the oven to 120°C (100°C fan/gas mark ½) and line a large baking tray with a silicone baking mat.

Place the plums and beetroot in a high-speed blender and blend for a couple of minutes until completely smooth.

Set a sieve over a bowl and tip in the plum purée, then work the mixture through the sieve with a spoon. Add honey to taste – if your plums are sweet you may not need much.

Tip the sieved mixture into a wide shallow saucepan or sauté pan over a medium to high heat and let it bubble away for 10 minutes, stirring regularly to prevent the mixture catching on the bottom of the pan. The idea is to lose as much moisture as possible before putting it in the oven. Be careful not to get burnt by the spluttering mixture!

Pour the mixture onto the silicone mat and level it out by tipping the tray until you have a thin, even layer.

Place the tray in the oven for 2 hours, then check if the mixture is ready by feeling it with your fingers: it should feel tacky but dry and not sticky. You can carefully have a go at peeling it off the silicone – if any sticky areas remain, put it back in the oven for another 20–30 minutes.

When ready, peel the fruit leather off the mat and cut it into strips or fun shapes with scissors. You can roll strips of the fruit leather up using paper and string to store them for packed lunches or snacks. They will keep in a dark, dry place for up to 2 months.

SPINACH + CUMIN FLATBREADS

15 MINS / **25 MINS** / **MAKES 6**

100g spinach, washed
250g natural yoghurt
300g plain flour, plus extra
 for dusting
2 tsp baking powder
1 tsp salt
2 tsp cumin seeds

Put the washed spinach in a microwavable bowl, cover and zap on high for 1½ minutes, or until well wilted, or wilt in a dry pan.

Put the yoghurt in a bowl with the spinach and blend with a stick blender until completely smooth and green.

Whisk the flour with the baking powder, salt and cumin seeds in a mixing bowl until well combined. Mix the green yoghurt into the flour with the stick end of a wooden spoon until the yoghurt is mixed into the flour. Next, go in with your hands and gently bring the dough together, adding in a little more flour if the dough feels too sticky.

Dust a clean work surface generously with flour. Tip the dough out onto the surface and divide it into 6 equal-sized pieces using a knife.

Dust the pieces of dough with flour then pat them out into round, thin flat shapes. Stack the shaped breads between layers of baking parchment to stop them from sticking.

Heat a large non-stick frying pan over a medium heat and cook the breads, one at a time, for a couple of minutes on each side, or until spotted golden brown and cooked through.

BRUSH THE FLATBREADS WITH BUTTER OR GHEE TO SERVE WITH CURRY OR HUMMUS.

CHILLI-STUFFED CHEESY PEPPERS

15 MINS / **40–45 MINS** / **FREEZE ME** / **SERVES 4** — 2 ADULTS + 2 SMALL KIDS

Preheat the oven to 220°C (200°C fan/gas mark 7).

Place the pepper halves cut side up in a baking dish large enough to accommodate them all in one layer, drizzle with 1 tablespoon of the olive oil and season with salt and pepper. Massage the peppers a little to evenly coat the inside and outside of the peppers with the oil and seasoning. Roast in the oven for 20 minutes until the peppers are starting to soften just a little.

Meanwhile, blitz the mushrooms in a food processor until finely chopped.

Heat the remaining olive oil in a large frying pan over a medium heat, add the mushrooms with a generous pinch of salt and cook for 15–20 minutes until all the water they release has evaporated and the mushrooms have turned mince-like in texture. Add the onion, minced beef, spices, garlic granules and dried oregano and cook for a further 5 minutes, breaking up the mince with a wooden spoon, until the mince is browned and the onion has softened. Stir in the tomato purée, add the orzo and stir in the beef stock. Simmer for 10 minutes, stirring from time to time, until the stock has been absorbed and the pasta is cooked. If the mixture becomes too dry you may need to add a splash of water. Stir in the kidney beans and cocoa powder and season with salt and pepper.

Preheat the grill to high.

Spoon the beef mince mixture into the cavities of the roasted pepper halves, sprinkle each pepper with some of the grated cheese and place under the grill for 3–4 minutes, or until the cheese is melted and bubbling golden brown.

Serve 4 half peppers per grown-up, and 2 per child.

6 peppers (red, yellow or orange), halved and deseeded
2 tbsp olive oil
salt and pepper
400g white or chestnut mushrooms, halved
1 large onion, finely chopped
350g minced beef
1 tsp sweet smoked paprika
1 tbsp ground cumin
½ tsp ground cinnamon
¼ tsp chilli powder
1 tsp garlic granules
1 tbsp dried oregano
2 tbsp tomato purée
150g orzo
500ml beef stock (made with 1 beef stock cube)
1 x 400g tin of kidney beans, drained
1 tsp cocoa powder
100g cheddar, grated

SALMON + SPINACH TRIANGULAR HAND PIES

20 MINS / **15–20 MINS** / **MAKES 4** SMALL

Preheat the oven to 200°C (180°C fan/gas mark 6) and line a baking tray with baking parchment.

Put the washed spinach in a microwaveable bowl, cover and zap on high for 2 minutes or until well wilted, or wilt it in a dry pan. Place the spinach in a sieve and press it with a spoon to remove as much water as possible. Roughly chop and leave to cool a little.

Dust a clean work surface with a little flour and roll out the pastry into a large square about the thickness of a pound coin.

Cut the square of puff pastry into quarters to form 4 smaller squares.

Mix the cooled spinach in a bowl with the lemon zest, cream cheese and chives, and season with a little salt and pepper.

Place the 4 squares of pastry on the lined tray and divide the cream cheese mixture and cubed salmon between the 4 squares of pastry, placing it towards the edge of one corner of each of the squares.

Use a pastry brush to brush the beaten egg around the edge of the pastry and then fold the opposite corner of pastry over the filling to form a triangular shape. Press the edges together with a fork and brush the tops with more egg wash.

Sprinkle the tops of the pies with the seeds (if using) then bake in the oven for 15–20 minutes until golden brown and cooked through.

Remove from the oven, let them cool a little (so the pies aren't too hot for little hands) and serve.

150g spinach, washed
plain flour, for dusting
500g block of puff pastry,
  remove it from the fridge
  20 minutes before needed
grated zest of 1 lemon
150g cream cheese
1 tbsp finely chopped chives
salt and pepper
1 x 350g skinless salmon fillet,
  cut into 4cm (1½in) cubes
1 egg, beaten
1 tbsp white sesame seeds –
  optional
1 tbsp nigella seeds – optional

SERVE WITH STEAMED GREEN BEANS + BROCCOLI

GET YOUR KIDS INVOLVED WITH MAKING THE PASTRY AND FILLING IT – THESE ARE GREAT FUN!

BEETROOT + BLUEBERRY PANCAKES

2 MINS / **5 MINS** / **FREEZE ME** / **MAKES 10**

100g porridge oats
2 eggs
100g cooked beetroot – not
 in vinegar (available in most
 supermarkets)
1 tsp baking powder
2 tbsp ground flaxseed
pinch of salt
100ml milk (dairy or
 plant-based)
coconut oil, for cooking
150g blueberries
honey, for drizzling

Put all of the ingredients, except the coconut oil, blueberries and honey, in a blender and blend for a couple of minutes until perfectly smooth.

Heat a little coconut oil in a non-stick frying pan over a medium heat. Spoon about 1 tablespoon of the batter into the pan and top the batter with a couple of blueberries. Cook for 1–2 minutes on each side, then continue cooking the remaining batter (you will use about half of the blueberries).

Serve the pancakes with the remaining blueberries and a drizzle of honey to serve.

TRY THESE WITH A BLOB OF YOGHURT, OR SWAP THE HONEY FOR MAPLE SYRUP.

PEAR, RASPBERRY + BEETROOT ICE LOLLIES

15 MINS / **NO COOK** / **MAKES 8** → *DEPENDING ON THE SIZE OF YOUR MOULDS*

↳ *PLUS 3-4 HOURS FREEZING*

1 ripe pear, peeled and cored
230g raspberries
200g cooked beetroot – not in vinegar (available in most supermarkets)
300g Greek yoghurt
juice of ½ lime
60ml maple syrup or honey

Put the fruit, beetroot and yoghurt in a blender and blend until perfectly smooth, then pass through a sieve into a bowl to remove the seeds from the raspberries. Get your child to help push the mixture through.

Mix the purée with the lime juice and maple syrup or honey. Tip the mixture into a jug, then pour into ice-lolly moulds and freeze (they will take at least 3–4 hours to freeze solid).

GET YOUR LITTLE ONE TO HELP FILL THE MOULDS.

PEAR, CRANBERRY + GINGER SEEDED GRANOLA

10 MINS / **35 MINS** / **15 SERVINGS**

2 ripe pears, cored and
 roughly chopped
 (no need to peel)
60ml maple syrup or honey
1 tbsp ground ginger
1 tsp ground cinnamon
60ml coconut oil, melted
400g porridge oats
70g pumpkin seeds
70g sunflower seeds
150g blanched almonds
100g dried cranberries

Preheat the oven to 180°C (160°C fan/gas mark 4) and line 2 baking trays with baking parchment.

Place the pears, maple syrup or honey, ground ginger, ground cinnamon and coconut oil in a blender and blend until perfectly smooth.

Place the oats, seeds and almonds in a mixing bowl. Pour in the pear mixture and stir to coat. The mixture will be quite wet and the oats will form clumps. Get your little ones to help with this.

Tip the mixture onto the lined baking trays, spreading it out into a single layer.

Bake in the oven for 20 minutes, then shuffle the mixture on the tray to help it brown evenly and place it back in the oven for another 15 minutes, or until golden brown and toasted.

Remove from the oven and mix the cranberries into the granola. Leave to cool, then tip into an airtight container.

SWEET POTATO WAFFLES

20 MINS / **5 MINS** / **MAKES 2-4**

2 LARGE WAFFLES OR 4 SMALL

↳ PER WAFFLE, PLUS SWEET POTATO COOKING TIME

Prick the sweet potato with a fork a couple of times, rinse under cold running water to dampen it a little and put in a microwavable bowl. Cover and zap on high for 8–10 minutes, or until perfectly soft and cooked through. Alternatively, cook the pricked sweet potato in the oven for 45 minutes at 220°C (200°C fan/gas mark 7).

Remove from the microwave and leave until it's cool enough to handle, then peel off and discard the skin. Chop the potato up a little, to release any steam and help it cool down quicker.

Place the oats in a blender or food processor and blitz to a flour-like consistency.

Push the potato through a potato ricer (if you have one) into a mixing bowl. If you don't have a potato ricer you can mash it with a fork until smooth.

Add the eggs, ground oats, baking powder, cinnamon, nutmeg and milk to the mashed sweet potato and stir well to combine.

Grease a waffle iron with a little coconut oil and heat until hot. Spoon in enough batter to fill, spreading it out a little with the back of a spoon. Cook for about 5 minutes until golden and cooked through. Continue until all the batter is used up.

1 large sweet potato (about 370g)
100g porridge oats
2 eggs, beaten
2 tsp baking powder
1 tsp ground cinnamon
¼ tsp freshly grated nutmeg
125ml oat milk
coconut oil, for greasing

YOU WILL NEED A WAFFLE IRON FOR THIS RECIPE.

SERVING SUGGESTIONS

- For a sweet treat, mix 30g tahini with 2 tablespoons of maple syrup then drizzle over the waffles and serve with a handful of blueberries. Get your little ones to help decorate the waffles.

- For a savoury option, top with fried eggs, sliced avocado, crispy bacon, grilled cherry tomatoes and a sprinkle of finely grated cheddar.

SPICED APPLE CRISPS

10 MINS / **40 MINS** / **MAKES 30** *APPROXIMATELY*

3 jazz apples
1 tsp ground cinnamon
1 tsp ground ginger

Preheat the oven to 140°C (120°C fan/gas mark 1) and line 2 large baking trays with baking parchment.

Slice the apples as thinly as you can with a sharp knife (use a mandoline if you have one, but be careful – it's very sharp, so not a tool for kids to use). There's no need to core or peel them.

Place the apple slices in a mixing bowl, sprinkle over the spices and gently toss to coat.

GET YOUR KIDS TO SPRINKLE OVER THE SPICES + TOSS THEM WITH THEIR HANDS TO COAT.

Lay the apple slices out in a single layer on the lined baking trays. Place in the oven and bake for 40 minutes, or until the apple slices have shrivelled slightly and crisped up.

Remove from the oven and leave to cool.

The crisps will keep in an airtight container for up to 1 week.

CELEBRATIONS

I'VE GOT YOU SORTED FOR SNACKS + TREATS!

PEANUT BUTTER POPCORN

2 MINS / 15 MINS / 1 LARGE BOWL

4 tsp coconut oil
100g popcorn kernels
3 tbsp maple syrup
4 tbsp smooth or crunchy
 peanut butter
pinch of salt

Preheat the oven to 180°C (160°C fan/gas mark 4) and line a large baking tray with baking parchment.

Melt 1 teaspoon of the coconut oil in a medium saucepan over a medium heat, and once the oil is hot, add the corn kernels in a single layer and place the lid on the pan.

After a minute or two the kernels will start popping. Give the pan a gentle shake back and forth, keeping the lid on and keeping it over the heat. Carefully lift the lid slightly (just a centimetre) to let some steam out, to make sure the popcorn stays crisp and doesn't go soggy.

When the popping sound becomes less frequent and there's a couple of seconds between pops, remove the pan from the heat. Remove the lid and tip the popcorn out onto the lined baking tray.

Add the remaining coconut oil, maple syrup, peanut butter and a pinch of salt to a small saucepan over a low heat and stir until combined and melted together.

Drizzle the peanut butter mixture over the popcorn and gently toss to coat the popcorn. Place in the oven for 3–4 minutes until the peanut butter mixture forms a dry crust on the popcorn. Tip into a big bowl and devour.

KEEP THE POPCORN SIMPLE IF YOU PREFER, OR JUST FLAVOUR IT WITH A DUSTING OF GROUND CINNAMON.

COURGETTE FRIES

20 MINS / 20–25 MINS / SERVES 3–4

olive oil spray
2 large courgettes (about 400g),
 cut into 1cm (½in)-wide batons
2 tbsp cornflour
salt and pepper
80g panko breadcrumbs
40g parmesan, grated
1½ tsp dried oregano
¼ tsp garlic granules
2 egg whites

Preheat the oven to 200°C (180°C fan/gas mark 6). Line a large baking tray with baking parchment and spray evenly with a little olive oil spray.

Pat the courgette batons dry with kitchen paper.

Place the cornflour on a plate and season with salt and pepper. Mix together the panko breadcrumbs, grated parmesan, oregano and garlic granules and place on another plate.

Whisk the egg whites a little in a small bowl until foamy.

Dust the courgette batons in the cornflour then dip in the egg whites and roll in the panko breadcrumbs to evenly coat. Place the courgettes on the prepared baking tray.

When all the courgettes batons are coated, spray the tops with the olive oil spray and bake in the oven for 20–25 minutes, or until golden brown and crispy.

Serve straight away.

THESE ARE LOVELY DIPPED IN KETCHUP.

SWEET POTATO CRISPS WITH PAPRIKA

10 MINS / 15–20 MINS / SERVES 2 — AS A SNACK

2 small sweet potatoes
2 tsp melted coconut oil
1 tsp sweet smoked paprika
 flakes
salt – optional

Preheat the oven to 180°C (160°C fan/gas mark 4) and line a large baking tray with baking parchment.

Cut the potatoes as thinly as possible into rounds, using a mandoline if you have one (leave the skin on).

Toss the sweet potato slices in the coconut oil to coat and sprinkle with the smoked paprika flakes, and a little salt (if using).

Lay the potato slices out in a single layer, making sure they don't overlap – if the tray isn't big enough, use two trays.

Bake in the oven for 15–20 minutes, flipping and shuffling the potatoes around on the tray halfway through the cooking time, until they are all crisp and starting to brown around the edges.

Remove from the oven and leave to cool before storing in an airtight container. They will keep for up to 2–3 days.

MARMITE + SPRING ONION CHEESE STRAWS

20 MINS / 25-30 MINS / FREEZE ME / MAKES 24

Preheat the oven to 200°C (180°C fan/gas mark 6) and line 2 baking trays with baking parchment.

Mix the Marmite in a small bowl with 1 teaspoon of hot water to loosen it a little so it has a more spreadable consistency.

Dust a work surface lightly with flour, then unwrap one sheet of the pastry onto the surface. Spread the pastry with the Marmite using the back of a spoon, until the entire surface of the pastry is covered. Sprinkle over the chopped spring onions, followed by half the cheese.

Unroll the second sheet of pastry and place it on top of the first sheet, matching up the corners.

Brush the top of the second sheet of pastry with beaten egg and sprinkle over the remaining cheese.

Using a rolling pin, and applying a light pressure, roll over the top of the two sheets so the cheese sticks to the pastry.

Using a sharp knife, cut the pastry into 1.5cm (⅝in)-thick strips and twist each strip gently, placing them on the lined baking trays as you go.

Bake in the oven for 25–30 minutes or until golden brown.

Remove from the oven and leave to cool a little before eating. They will keep for up to 1 week in an airtight container.

To freeze, freeze raw straws on a lined baking tray and cook from frozen, adding 10 minutes to the cooking time.

5 tsp Marmite
plain flour, for dusting
2 x 320g sheets of puff pastry
6 spring onions, finely chopped
200g cheddar, finely grated
1 egg, beaten

THESE ARE GREAT SERVED EITHER WARM OR COLD.

AVOCADO MINT CHOC CHIP ICE CREAM

15 MINS / NO COOK / SERVES 6–8

+ 4 HOURS FREEZING

3 perfectly ripe avocados,
de-stoned and peeled
2 tsp peppermint extract
2 x 160ml tins of coconut cream
150ml maple syrup or agave
syrup
juice of 2 limes
100g dark chocolate
mint leaves, to decorate –
optional

Put the avocado flesh, peppermint extract, coconut cream, maple or agave syrup and lime juice in a food processor or blender and blitz until smooth.

Tip the mixture into a shallow freezer-proof container (ideally metal, as this will help it freeze quicker).

Place the blended avocado mixture in the freezer along with the chocolate (still in its wrapper) for 2 hours. Take the chocolate out of the freezer and hit it with a rolling pin to break it into small pieces – I usually leave the chocolate in its wrapper to do this. Remove the avocado mixture from the freezer and mix the broken chocolate through it. Return it to the freezer for another 2 hours, or until frozen. You may need to take the ice cream out of the freezer and leave it at room temperature for 10–15 minutes to soften a little before scooping into bowls or cones. Decorate with mint leaves, if you like.

BLACK CHERRY + YOGHURT RIPPLE ICE CREAM

15 MINS / NO COOK / SERVES 6–8

+ 4 HOURS FREEZING

Put the double cream, 100ml of the maple syrup and the vanilla bean paste in a large mixing bowl and whisk with a handheld electric whisk until the mixture forms soft peaks. Fold in the Greek yoghurt until fully combined and pour into a wide, shallow freezer-safe container. Freeze the mixture for 3–4 hours, or until completely frozen.

Place the frozen black cherries in a food processor with the remaining maple syrup and lemon juice and blitz until smooth. Empty into a bowl and clean the bowl of the food processor.

Chop the frozen Greek yoghurt into smaller blocks, place in the food processor and process until smooth.

Tip the blended Greek yoghurt mixture back into the freezer-safe container.

Ripple the frozen cherry mixture through the frozen Greek yoghurt mixture with a spoon and place back in the freezer for 20–30 minutes until frozen enough to scoop.

Scoop into cones or bowls to serve.

300ml double cream
180ml maple syrup
1 tsp vanilla bean paste
500g Greek yoghurt
320g frozen dark cherries
juice of ½ lemon

TRY SWAPPING THE BLACK CHERRIES FOR MIXED FROZEN BERRIES.

THIS IS GREAT WITH CHOCOLATE GRATED OVER IT.

CHOCOLATE, PRUNE + AVOCADO MOUSSE WITH CHERRIES

20 MINS / NO COOK / SERVES 4

+ CHILLING TIME

60g dark chocolate, broken
 into pieces
3 ripe avocados, de-stoned
 and peeled
1 banana, peeled
8 prunes, soaked in hot water
 for 10 minutes to soften,
 then drained
2 tbsp cocoa powder
pinch of salt
3–4 tbsp maple syrup
100g fresh cherries (or other
 seasonal soft red fruit such
 as raspberries or strawberries),
 to serve

Melt the chocolate in a heatproof bowl placed over a pan of gently simmering water (making sure the bottom of the bowl doesn't touch the water).

Put the avocado flesh in a food processor with the peeled banana, soaked prunes, melted chocolate, cocoa powder, salt and 3 tablespoons of the maple syrup. Blend until smooth, taste a little of the mixture and add more maple syrup if you prefer a sweeter flavour.

Spoon into 4 decorative glasses or bowls, transfer to the fridge to chill for 10–15 minutes and serve with cherries or other soft berries.

COCONUT JELLIES WITH RASPBERRY SAUCE

20 MINS / 3 MINS / MAKES 4

↳ + 2–3 HOURS SETTING TIME

5 gelatine leaves
400ml coconut milk
250ml coconut cream
2 tsp vanilla extract
60ml maple syrup
250g frozen (and defrosted)
 or fresh raspberries
20g coconut flakes
1 heaped tsp dark brown sugar
1 tsp lime juice

Put the gelatine leaves in a small bowl, cover with cold water and leave to soak for 10 minutes.

Place the coconut milk and cream in a small saucepan and heat through until hot. Stir in the vanilla extract and maple syrup and remove from the heat.

Squeeze any excess water from the gelatine leaves and whisk them into the coconut milk until dissolved.

Pour the mixture into 4 decorative glasses, ramekins or small jelly moulds and place in the fridge for 2–3 hours until set.

Blend the raspberries in a jug or bowl with a stick blender until smooth, then pass through a sieve to remove the seeds.

Toast the coconut flakes in a small frying pan over a low heat for a couple of minutes until golden. Add the brown sugar and lime juice and heat for 1 minute until coated. Remove from the heat.

Turn the jellies out onto plates (if using moulds) and serve the jellies with the raspberry sauce and toasted coconut.

BEETROOT + CHOCOLATE CAKE WITH CHOCOLATE AVOCADO BUTTERCREAM

30 MINS / **35 MINS** / **SERVES 10–12**

Preheat the oven to 180°C (160°C fan/gas mark 4). Grease two 22cm (8in) springform cake tins with a little coconut oil and line the bases with baking parchment.

Melt the chocolate in a heatproof bowl placed over a pan of gently simmering water (making sure the bottom of the bowl doesn't touch the water). Remove from the heat and set aside.

Blitz the cooked beetroot in a food processor or in a jug or bowl with a stick blender until it is fairly smooth and no large lumps remain (a bit of texture is fine). Set aside.

Put the eggs, vanilla extract, melted coconut oil and coconut sugar in a stand mixer fitted with a whisk attachment and beat on a medium speed for 3–4 minutes (or in a bowl with an electric handheld whisk) until thoroughly combined and the mixture looks creamy and smooth.

Sift the flour, cacao powder, baking powder and bicarbonate of soda into the bowl and fold in with a wooden spoon. Fold in the beetroot and chocolate and mix until fully combined. Divide the mixture evenly between the lined cake tins and bake for 35 minutes, or until a skewer inserted into the middle of the cakes comes out clean.

Remove from the oven and leave to cool in the tins for at least 30 minutes, then remove and place on wire racks to cool completely. While the cakes are cooling, make the buttercream.

Blend the avocados in a food processor or in a jug or bowl with a stick blender until smooth, then add the maple syrup and cacao powder and blend again until combined.

Level off the tops of the cooled cakes using a serrated knife. Spread half the buttercream on one of the cakes and sandwich the second cake on top. Spread the remaining buttercream over the top and decorate as you wish.

FOR THE CAKE

200ml melted coconut oil, plus extra for greasing
200g dark chocolate, broken into pieces
500g cooked beetroot (not in vinegar)
6 eggs
2 tbsp vanilla extract
200g coconut sugar
200g self-raising flour
100g cacao powder
1 tsp baking powder
1 tsp bicarbonate of soda

FOR THE CHOCOLATE AVOCADO BUTTERCREAM

2 large ripe avocados, de-stoned and peeled (250g prepared weight)
4 tbsp maple syrup
4 tbsp cacao powder

TO DECORATE

Decorate the cake as you fancy, maybe with grated chocolate or chocolate curls, fresh strawberries, raspberries or cherries and a sprinkling of chopped toasted hazelnuts

PICTURED OVERLEAF →

BEETROOT + CHOCOLATE CAKE
WITH CHOCOLATE AVOCADO
BUTTERCREAM

CARAMELIZED BANANAS WITH ICE CREAM + TOASTED NUTS

5 MINS / 5 MINS / SERVES 4

2 ADULTS + 2 SMALL KIDS

2 tbsp date syrup (or honey or maple syrup)

½ tsp cocoa powder

4 bananas, peeled and halved lengthways

4 tsp soft dark brown sugar

½ lemon

4 scoops of cherry and Greek yoghurt ice cream (see page 219) or shop-bought ice cream of your choice

40g toasted hazelnuts, roughly chopped

4 fresh cherries, to decorate – optional, halved and pitted for little kids

Preheat the grill to its hottest setting.

Whisk the date syrup with the cocoa powder in a bowl.

Place the bananas on a baking tray cut side up and sprinkle the brown sugar over the bananas. Squeeze a little lemon juice on each banana and place under the grill for 2–3 minutes, or until the sugar has melted and the bananas are nicely caramelized.

Place the caramelized banana halves onto plates or bowls (2 per serving) and top with the ice cream of your choice. Drizzle over the sauce and sprinkle with the nuts. Decorate with fresh cherries (if using) to serve.

INDEX

ACKNOWLEDGEMENTS

To the sunshine in my life, Rosie, Marley and Indie. I love that we are here together growing up and learning from each other every day. I can't wait to look back on this book in a few years, Marley and Indie, and tell you how cheeky you both were on the photoshoot.

This is my tenth book and I have to say I actually love this one the most because it's the first book we are all in together. I absolutely love the photography and food styling, too. Every recipe looks unreal. Thank you Andrew, Natalie and Katie for your incredible creativity.

Thank you so much Carole and everyone at Bluebird for always investing in the best people to help create the most beautiful books. A book like this takes so much teamwork and energy and I'm so incredibly grateful for being able to work with you all. I will always be so thankful for the opportunity you gave me to create books. What a journey it's been.

MUCH LOVE, JOE X

the body coach

SAY HELLO TO A REAL GAME CHANGER

The Body Coach app
OUT NOW

Continue your journey at thebodycoach.com